79
C
fu
P
7(

D0176792

VE MAR 2008 13

coaching
KIDS' SOCCER

This book is dedicated to Heidi, Aimée and Chris for putting up with my absolute passion for soccer

Acknowledgments

I would like to acknowledge the following people and organizations for their help and support:

Peter Page; Charles Mortimore MBE; the FA; the NSPCC; the team at A&C Black; the staff of Badshot Lea FC, Farnborough Town FC and Reading FC; Sparsholt and South Downs colleges.

Stuart Page

coaching
KIDS' SOCCER
Fun, safe and positive soccer for all ages

FIREFLY BOOKS

A FIREFLY BOOK

Published by Firefly Books Ltd. 2008

Copyright © 2008 Stuart Page

All rights reserved. No part of this publication may be reproduced, stored in a retrieval system, or transmitted in any form or by any means, electronic, mechanical, photocopying, recording or otherwise, without the prior written permission of the Publisher.

First printing

Publisher Cataloging-in-Publication Data (U.S.)

Page, Stuart, 1962–
      Coaching kids' soccer : fun, safe and positive soccer for all ages / Stuart Page.
[240] p. : ill., photos. ;   cm.
Includes index.
Summary: Handbook for coaches, teachers and parents to organizing, running and managing youth soccer. Covers topics including: child protection and safety, mental and physical development, codes of conduct, sample coaching sessions, psychology and nutrition.
ISBN-13: 978-1-55407-354-2 (pbk.)
ISBN-10: 1-55407-354-5 (pbk.)
1. Soccer for children—Coaching. I. Title.
796.33407   dc22   GV943.8P343   2008

Library and Archives Canada Cataloguing in Publication

Page, Stuart, 1962–
      Coaching kids' soccer : fun, safe and positive soccer for all ages / Stuart Page.
Includes index.
ISBN-13: 978-1-55407-354-2
ISBN-10: 1-55407-354-5
      1. Soccer for children—Coaching. I. Title.
GV943.8.P33 2008   796.33407'7   C2007-904197-3

Published in the United States by
Firefly Books (U.S.) Inc.
P.O. Box 1338, Ellicott Station
Buffalo, New York 14205

Published in Canada by
Firefly Books Ltd.
66 Leek Crescent
Richmond Hill, Ontario L4B 1H1

Cover design Erin R. Holmes
Interior design James Wakelin
Illustrations Dave Saunders, Andrée Jenks

Printed in Great Britain

contents

Photograph © Stéphane Rocher 2007

Stuart Page has over 35 years experience in football, as a player, coach and official. A full member of the Football Association (FA) Coaches Association, Stuart is at Union of European Football Association (UEFA) "A" Licence level and a qualified FA Coach Educator. He also has over 20 years commercial business experience, having successfully set up and run his own IT consultancy practice. He currently lectures in sports studies at The South Downs college in Hampshire, England.

Between 1993 and 2007, Stuart was the Head Coach & Chairman of Badshot Lea Football Club (FC), based in Surrey, where he was also a Child Protection and Welfare Officer. During his tenure as Chairman, Stuart led the development of the club from very humble beginnings to becoming one of the largest junior grassroots clubs in the United Kingdom, running over 25 teams for boys, girls and adults. The club also received the prestigious FA Charter Standard Community Club status and boasts a FA National Volunteer of Year among its management team. From 2004 to 2007, Stuart also coached and managed the Reserve and U18 Youth side at Farnborough Town FC before joining Havant & Waterloovile FC as Head of their Youth Football Academy.

Stuart lives in Hampshire with his wife, Heidi, and their two children, Aimée and Christopher.

Foreword

Charles Mortimore at Buckingham Palace, receiving his MBE in recognition of services to young people in sport (photo courtesy of Charles Mortimore)

I first met Stuart Page in 2000 when his son, Chris, was selected for the Hampshire District Representative team. I immediately recognized Stuart's deep-rooted passion for the game and found him to be a professional and dedicated assistant manager whenever I needed a highly qualified coach to run a District Representative side for me.

Stuart is an approachable and open-minded individual who possesses a sound knowledge of the game. It is of no surprise to me, therefore, that he has written a reference book to help transfer his wealth of coaching experience to teachers and coaches coming into the game. Stuart is also one of those rare people in the game who serves soccer development without any hidden agendas or for any selfish gain. He is honest and loyal to players, passionate about the game, committed to soccer's long-term development and firmly behind coaching good practices. Above all, Stuart has never wavered from his three key principles of the competent coach – for players to be safe, have fun and be inspired. *Coaching Kids' Soccer* will be a lifelong legacy to his principles, which I totally subscribe to.

It is fair to say that I have enjoyed a long life in and around sport, in particular around young sporting hopefuls. My own soccer career saw me play at the very top of the amateur levels. Once qualified as a physical education teacher at Loughborough University, where I captained the soccer side to the national university championship, I was called up to the Royal Air Force (RAF) for a two year stint. On leaving the RAF, my "serious" football career began in earnest with Aldershot in the Football League (South) where I was a prolific goalscorer, notching five goals in one very memorable game against Leyton Orient. I then joined Woking, where the highlight for me was leading them to victory in the 1950 Amateur FA Cup Final at the old Wembley stadium in front of 71,000 spectators. The fact that it was on my birthday, and that the crowd all sang "Happy Birthday" to me, made it particularly special. As a player, I was fortunate to receive 20 caps for England Amateurs, including being the only ever-present player in a pro/am England side that successfully toured Ghana and Nigeria.

After hanging the boots up, I carried on teaching at Cove School in Hampshire during which time I continued to identify and develop young local talented soccer players, helping many become professional players. In 2001, I was immensely humbled yet proud to be rewarded with an MBE (Member of the Order of the British Empire) in recognition of my services to young people in sport.

I enthusiastically welcome any quality guide to good practice in the game and I am convinced *Coaching Kids' Soccer* will join the list of invaluable coaching reference. There is a plethora of tactical and technical resources available to coaches, but I found it particularly refreshing to see that *Coaching Kids' Soccer* directly provides a comprehensive, yet easy-to-follow guide for the inexperienced, non-soccer-qualified teacher and coach. The book gives invaluable advice on good practice for anyone involved with young soccer players, offering comprehensive and sound guides on health and safety, child protection, preparation and delivery of coaching, with plenty of very useful and easy-to-run drills. This is of paramount importance these days because it is these inexperienced teachers and coaches who are responsible for children that are in their "golden age" of learning and who are our future stars of the game. If we can get the coaching right at this early stage of their development, we might just produce a few more homegrown talented sports stars tomorrow.

CHARLES MORTIMORE, MBE

Introduction

Is there anything more delightful than watching children immerse themselves in an activity that is stimulating, progressive and enjoyable, in which they can achieve a level of success that surpasses even their expectations? The delight increases tenfold if the activity also helps to develop good social skills and continued health and fitness.

Although you could list a plethora of activities that fit this category, perhaps the one that springs to mind is sports, and soccer in particular. Soccer is enjoyed by hundreds of millions of people around the world, none more so than children under the age of 18. Although the vast majority of children will never play competitive soccer at a professional level, many will play regularly – socially and recreationally – throughout their formative years at school, often at an organized junior club. They will carry what they learn in adolescence into adult life so it is important that anyone responsible for shaping and guiding their learning should do it to the very best of their ability and to the highest standard.

Soccer is a growing sport in North America. It is one of the most watched sports in the world, it has a huge number of participants and a great deal of financial investment. It should therefore come as no surprise that the governing bodies of soccer are on a constant crusade to implement and maintain high standards of quality and safety. They aim to do this by encouraging, supporting, informing and educating all those involved in football, or considering getting involved.

Did you know that in the United States:

- Over 3 million children between the ages of 5 and 19 play in registered soccer leagues?
- Around 14 million Americans aged seven years and older play soccer more than once a year?
- Over 900,000 adults, including some 300,000 coaches, are involved in youth soccer?

This book gives you all the information you need to organize successful soccer. Whether you are a passionate volunteer, a schoolteacher or qualified coach, *Coaching Kids' Soccer* will take you step by step through forming, maintaining and developing young players and teams in a structured, safe and sound manner.

Above all, *Coaching Kids' Soccer* will provide you with ample guidance and points of reference to ensure that safety, enjoyment and protection are placed highest on the agenda. It aims to help everyone involved in soccer to develop and implement the necessary good habits and practices to preserve this beautiful game for centuries to come.

Many children enjoy the game but show no natural skill or ability. These children may be neglected or expected to keep up with the more gifted players by coaches and teachers, which often leads to exclusion. This need not be the case, however, and with good practice parents, teachers, coaches and other organizers can make soccer fun, healthy, enjoyable and character-building for everyone participating, regardless of their size, age, ability and level of maturity. Coaches can have a dramatically positive influence on a young person's life if, from the start, a policy of good practice, care and attention is adopted.

At the club level, the majority of junior soccer around the world is administered by passionate volunteers who have no formal training or qualifications. When managing children and children's activities, it is vital that adults are well-informed. Sadly, the emphasis on good practice is often overshadowed by the desire to produce superstars. As such, the important aspects of safety, fun, progressive learning and natural development are all too often overlooked, and the needs of less gifted participants neglected. It is therefore vitally important that parents, teachers and coaches are given the same level of help and support that we expect them to give our children. Our children may be the future but it is the adults who guide them and ensure that good practice is maintained and developed.

My involvement in junior/grassroots football has given me the knowledge and experience to get things right, to recognize and act when things are going wrong and to ensure that the children we are responsible for grow up to love the game to which we introduce them. I hope I bring all of this experience and passion to the pages of *Coaching Kids' Soccer*. As head coach I have been responsible for turning enthusiastic parents into competent and qualified coaches. This has not always been easy, as gaining qualifications is not high on everyone's priority list. However, this issue is quickly resolved when I ask parents how they would feel if someone who refused to obtain appropriate coaching and child protection qualifications was responsible for coaching their children.

In this book I have included chapters on risk assessment, preparation for activity and actions to take in the event of emergencies. There are plenty of coaching drills relative to age, level of maturity and physical development, with additional guides on how to make soccer educational without losing the fun, enjoyment and health and safety aspects. The book is designed to cover the many situations coaches, parents and teachers will face as they help guide soccer-loving children's journeys to adulthood. I hope you enjoy the book and will derive benefit from it for many years to come.

STUART PAGE

part 1

AN INTRODUCTION
TO COACHING

chapter 1
LAYING THE FOUNDATIONS

There is no doubt about it: a safe and enjoyable coaching and playing environment, such as a well-run soccer club, can have a profound and positive social impact on its members and the local community, especially the children. It can create, shape and develop a good sense of responsibility, respect, care and welfare among all.

The good practice guidelines that clubs and schools now have to adopt do have a powerful effect on young players who have to embrace and uphold the standards or risk being excluded. I have seen the most street-hardened and aggressive individuals, who show an alarming disrespect and disregard on day one, do a U-turn in their attitude and general demeanor after a short while, displaying a real passion for their club and care for others within it.

Codes of conduct at most clubs make provision for all user groups: teachers, coaches and managers, players, officials, parents, members and spectators. These common-sense guidelines lay out the behavior and values expected by the club, and exist to protect the interests of the club and its members. They are there to say to anyone wishing to break the rules that they are not welcome and that their social skills and levels of respect are unacceptable. So, even before a ball is kicked members sign up to a set of rules that will ensure a high level of behavior.

Players, especially at youth ages, can display a quite shocking lack of respect toward whatever is provided for them and those who provide it. Yet these attitudes can quickly be changed for the better through the pleasure of playing a game they love, the discipline of teamwork and the benefits of hard work. It is the thought of having these withdrawn because of their poor levels of respect, commitment and general social graces that really wakes up disruptive and misbehaving individuals.

A controversial point maybe, but it is arguable that a well-run soccer club has a greater social impact than perhaps a school classroom or workplace might, in so much as the environment is recreational, sociable and is there to fuel fun and enjoyment in a sport its participants and members love.

Soccer teams and clubs can only provide good social environments if they are well run. Organizations such as U.S. Youth Soccer, the American Youth Soccer Organization (AYSO) and the various provincial soccer associations in Canada provide the necessary framework for players, parents and coaches. Further development is offered at the elite level through the U.S. Soccer Development Academy. These organizations operate under general rules not only for how the games are played and the competitions run, but also for how the players and coaches should behave.

As a well-run soccer club brings so many benefits to its members and the local community, it is essential that those involved in running the clubs lay a good, solid foundation. They need to establish a baseline of discipline and rules that clearly lays out the high standards of behavior, attitudes, ethics and values expected of members and participants, but which also maintains maximum fun, enjoyment and safety.

Benefits of Affiliation with a Soccer Organization

Organizations such as U.S. Youth Soccer, AYSO, the Canadian Soccer Association and the various Canadian provincial soccer associations have set standards for coaching, administration and child protection. Working and playing within these structures improves the experience for all. To be blunt, my advice to parents seeking a safe and quality-driven environment for their children is to find a club that is affiliated with a recognized soccer authority and ensure their child is being coached in an environment where a stringent child protection policy is in place and where all the coaches are qualified in coaching and emergency first aid. To find out more visit www.usyouthsoccer.org, www.soccer.org or the Canadian Soccer Association at www.canadasoccer.com, which has a complete list of provincial associations.

So, such ground rules are vital and should be in place before anyone at your club kicks a ball. This way, everyone – and rules are not just for players but for members, officials, coaches, parents and other spectators alike – knows what is acceptable or unacceptable behavior, and is aware of the potential consequences if the rules are not adhered to; put simply, this will be the withdrawal of benefits for those who do not respect the code.

There are a number of organizations that can give guidance on good practice and goal-setting, as well as offering financial support to community projects. I have detailed some of these organizations later on in this chapter. First, here are some guidelines on areas you should consider when drawing up your standards of good practice, based on my experiences.

Attitude and Ethics

The basic principles to uphold are fair play and overall participation, not the result of the game. There is nothing unhealthy about wanting to win – soccer would be nothing without its competitive nature – but there are ways and means of expressing yourself in the face of victory or defeat.

Players

Players need to learn self-discipline and the fundamentals of fair play to ensure that everyone gets the most out of playing soccer. Though young people might regularly see examples of bad behavior from players at soccer fields and in televised games, they need to learn that such behavior will not be put up with at any level! As with any sport, soccer governing bodies take a dim view of such antics and so should you.

Self-control

- Getting angry and/or crying when losing or having lost are unacceptable behaviors, even if only directed at yourself. This only has a negative impact on other people and should be kept in check;
- Taking out one's frustrations on someone else is also unacceptable, be it a team-mate who has made a mistake or a referee whose decision is disagreed with.
- You should remember that verbal abuse, telling someone that they are no good or making threatening remarks are every bit as harmful as physical bullying or intimidation.
- Spitting at any other person is disrespectful, disgraceful and insulting.
- Any form of physical contact intended to cause harm to another person must not and will not be tolerated.

Fair play

- Targeting individual opposing players, either physically (e.g., by persistent, deliberate fouling) or verbally (insults/threats) to try and gain advantage is against the spirit of fair play and must not be tolerated.
- "Play acting," e.g., feigning injury to try and get an opposing player sent off or falsely reporting an incident to an official, is as bad in its own way as a professional foul or a verbal insult.
- Players should act respectfully toward their opponents, shake hands with them at the end of the game and say "well done," whether this be accepting defeat graciously or showing empathy in victory. Remember that without the opposition, there could be no game.
- Players should not brag or gloat in victory, especially in front of the opposition.

Coaches

It is essential to appreciate that a coach is not just there to teach young people soccer skills, and that coaching staff have a duty of care to the youngsters they are coaching. Do not underestimate the influence coaches' actions could have on young people and how they conduct themselves. Below are common mistakes for coaches to avoid and alternative actions, followed by a list of competencies you should adopt for a code of conduct that ensures better coaching and mentoring at your club.

Coaching principles – Do's and don'ts

- Do show commitment to the team, but channel energy positively, even when things are not going well on the field.
- Don't argue with officials if you disagree with their actions – this will only legitimize this kind of behavior in your players' eyes.
- Do try and establish a good relationship with your players from the beginning and be as warm and approachable as possible so they will respect you.
- Do set down basic ground rules, but don't "lay down the law" or be too inflexible in your approach.
- Do make sure you are consistent – don't break your own rules or make exceptions for certain individuals.
- Don't withdraw players from activities for disciplinary reasons, as isolation of individuals will probably cause more problems.

- Do use positive reinforcement within the structure of your activities to discipline players who break the rules.
- Don't be hard on players who "underperform."
- Don't overpromote or overuse skillful players, or place them on a pedestal.
- Do use praise, but only with justification.
- Don't shame less talented players by making an example of their mistakes or by comparing them to more skillful individuals.
- Do consider that players of varying skill levels can play together.
- Do remember that every young person is an individual who might be more or less sensitive to criticism, constructive or otherwise.
- Do take note that if you pick on a particular young person and criticize them publicly, others might see this as a license to continue to abuse or ridicule the individual when you are no longer there.
- Do listen to your players – if you need to change things at half-time or mid-season, allow the team to have their say and make constructive and positive comments to you and one another in an objective way. They might think of something you hadn't considered.

Coaching competencies

Below are some of the attributes a good coach needs to tailor activities to everyone's advantage, with some advice and examples of positive outcomes from my experiences:

Responsive

I've had teams where individual players have told me that they find a certain skill exercise too hard, for example. Consider whether the activity you're doing is beneficial depending on the age and skill level of all the participants and adapt accordingly. Be a problem-solver; innovate and improvise.

Accountable

Remember that as well as the responsibilities of a duty of care to your players and looking after your own interests, you owe it to your colleagues to reflect the effort they put into assisting you with activities. Your role is as much about the continued development of soccer in the community as it is teaching soccer skills, so a lot of people are relying on you.

Courageous

You are there to set standards, so be brave and aim high! Make the quality of your coaching raise the bar for performance; do it without fear, as long as you feel it's right for the game and is realistically attainable by everyone involved with what you're trying to achieve. Be open to new suggestions, and make sure you give credit and assurances to encourage players and other people at your club to take responsibility. You'll be amazed at how a few words of positive encouragement will motivate people to help you. I couldn't have developed the clubs I've been involved with through my individual efforts alone.

Inclusive

Within reason, rotate your squad! Reflect your players' enthusiasm and commitment by giving them an equal share of opportunities. Be careful to reassure "dropped" players that they are still in with a shout and encourage them to train hard with the rest of the team. If a player is on the subs' bench, try to make sure you use them.

Passionate

You are a role model – if you love the game and show it, you will make the young people in your charge do the same.

Organized

Use your knowledge in a focused way and have goals to achieve standards. Make sure when you are coaching that the players understand why you are doing an activity and what you are aiming to achieve. Don't use complicated language, especially when explaining things to younger players. Remember that children will have been inspired to play soccer by watching their favorite teams and players, and even older siblings, without necessarily knowing all the rules.

Code of Conduct

Hopefully you will now have a good idea of the kind of standards and codes of practice required by a well-run soccer club. Taking this a step further, the United States Soccer Federation, U.S. Youth Soccer, AYSO, the Canadian Soccer Association and the various Canadian provincial soccer associations apply codes of conduct. These set positive standards to adhere to, and reject negatives.

There are codes for coaches, players, officials and other relevant parties, including parents. For more details see www.ussoccer.com, www.usyouthsoccer.org, www.soccer.org and www.canadasoccer.com.

Anti-discrimination and Equal Opportunities

The United States and Canada are ethnically and culturally diverse countries, and soccer is an international game. Instilling a sense of equality into young people at the earliest age possible is therefore essential. Naturally, the United States Soccer Federation and the Canadian Soccer Association actively promote equal opportunities, but they are not the only organizations involved in educating people on the need for equality of opportunity at all levels of soccer and assisting community projects. This section details some useful sources of help, information and inspiration when you are considering diversity and equal opportunities at your club.

Racism

While sports have undoubtedly come a long way since the days of racial segregation, racial discrimination does still exist in sports and society, and soccer is no exception. Many national team players of color have reported being subjected to racial slurs, by both other players and fans. Following FIFA's international lead in combating racism, there are a number of community initiatives that target inappropriate behavior.

International Anti-discrimination Policies

FIFA, soccer's world governing body, has recognized its unique role in coordinating opinions and expertise from all corners of the globe to share experiences and to find effective solutions to problems relating to discrimination and social integration.

Programs like Football for Hope and FIFA Ambassadors against Racism aim to show that soccer belongs to, and should be enjoyed by, everyone equally. The objective is to eliminate discrimination, whether by reason of gender, sexual orientation, race, nationality, ethnic origin, color, religion or ability, and to encourage equal opportunities. Such policies should be at the heart of every club's, school's and community's activities. Visit www.fifa.com for more information about FIFA's social responsibility programs.

In the United States, the National Collegiate Athletic Association (NCAA) is deeply committed to combating racism in sports. Its Diversity and Inclusion Department operates a variety of programs – for both players and coaches – aimed at enhancing and encouraging diversity and inclusion throughout intercollegiate athletics. The NCAA also offers sportsmanship tool kits intended for younger athletes, which outline best practices for administrators, coaches, student athletes, trainers, officials, fans and spirit-booster groups. Visit www.ncaa.org for more information and to download toolkits.

In Canada, campaigns such as the Quebec soccer federation's "no to racism on my field" aim to stamp out racism at all levels of soccer. Further to FIFA's 2001 Conference Against Racism, all members of Quebec's soccer federation – players, coaches, referees and volunteers – are being encouraged to sign a "no to racism on my field" declaration to formalize their commitment to combat racism in soccer.

Players with Disabilities

The United States Soccer Federation and the Canadian Soccer Association agree that children's soccer should be first and foremost about having fun and should include all children, including those with disabilities. As a result, both U.S.

Youth Soccer and the American Youth Soccer Organization have programs designed to bring disabled and special-needs children into soccer. In addition to the programs outlined below, the Special Olympics feature soccer and provide year-round training and competitions in a variety of sports for children and adults with intellectual disabilities through more than 200 programs in 160 countries worldwide (visit www.specialolympics.org). The U.S.A. Deaf Soccer Association also fields both men's and women's teams at the Deaflympics (visit www.usdeafsoccer.com).

TOPSoccer

U.S. Youth Soccer's The Outreach Program for Soccer (TOPSoccer) is a community-based training and team-placement program for young athletes with disabilities. Organized by volunteers, the program is designed to bring the opportunity to learn and play soccer to any boy or girl who has a mental or physical disability. The goal is to enable the young athletes with disabilities to become valued and successful soccer players. For information about this program visit www.usyouthsoccer.org.

Very Important Players

The American Youth Soccer Organization's Very Important Players (VIP) program aims to provide a quality soccer experience for children and adults whose physical or mental disabilities make it difficult for them to successfully participate on mainstream teams. The program recognizes that all children need to feel a sense of belonging and acceptance, and it embodies AYSO's philosophy of "Everyone Plays."

These VIPs include children who are blind or visually impaired, amputees, mobility impaired, autistic and mentally or emotionally challenged, and kids who have cerebral palsy. You can visit www.soccer.org/Programs/VIP to find out more about VIP.

Soccer Ability League

The National Sports Center for the Disabled developed the Soccer Ability League in partnership with U.S. Paralympics to encourage individuals with physical disabilities to play soccer. Teams participate in organized local leagues, and the program focuses on ambulatory athletes with physical challenges such as cerebral palsy, stroke, muscle disorders, traumatic brain injury, spina bifida and leg amputations. At the time of publication, the Soccer Ability League is operating in seven U.S. cities, and there are plans to expand to more cities in the near future. For more information visit the National Sports Center's website at www.nscd.org.

Canadian Programs

The Active Living Alliance for Canadians with a Disability works to promote, support and enable Canadians with disabilities to lead active and healthy lives. Their website, www.ala.ca, provides information on soccer and other sports events happening across Canada, and lists a number of sports-related resources for disabled Canadians.

Through its provincial affiliates, the Canadian Cerebral Palsy Sports Association operates CP Soccer, a slightly modified version of the traditional game for athletes with cerebral palsy. Visit www.ccpsa.ca for more information.

Girls and Soccer

Given the continued success of the national American and Canadian women's soccer teams – particularly in comparison to their male counterparts – and with stars such as Mia Hamm and Kristine Lilly to look up to, it's no surprise that soccer is a popular sport among girls of all ages in North America. However, the possibility of sexual discrimination is always a concern, and a well-organized soccer club will make sure that girls are never sidelined.

The President's Challenge is a series of programs overseen and funded by the U.S. government that are designed to help improve the activity levels of men and women of all ages. Among these initiatives are publications that focus on girls' fitness, demonstrating the positive impact sports can have on a girl's life. These publications can be downloaded from the President's Challenge website at www.fitness.gov.

Both the United States and Canada also have associations that aim to help keep girls active and involved in sports – the National Association for Girls and Women in Sport and the Canadian Association for the Advancement of Women and Sport and Physical Activity. Information about the initiatives these associations run and fund can be found on their websites, www.aahperd.org/nagws and www.caaws.ca.

Homophobia

It is estimated that between two and ten percent of the population is homosexual, yet openly gay players, coaches and other people involved in the national game are virtually non-existent. As a coach you should consider introducing an anti-homophobia section to any codes of conduct at your club to encourage participation of people of all sexual orientations, be they coaches or young people.

It Takes a Team!

It Takes A Team! is an educational campaign for lesbian, gay, bisexual and transgender issues in sport run by the Women's Sports Foundation. The project focuses on eliminating homophobia as a barrier to not just all women but also to all men participating in sport. The primary goals are to develop and disseminate practical educational information and resources to athletic administrators, coaches, parents, and athletes at the high school and college levels. To that end, a wealth of information can be found on their website, www.womenssportsfoundation.org/cgi-bin/iowa/issues/itat/index.html. The site features an education kit, a guide for handling anti-gay harassment and action guides for coaches, parents and athletes. Free stickers and posters can also be ordered through the site.

Gay and Lesbian Athletes Association

A registered charity operating in both the United States and Canada, GLAA's goal is to create an atmosphere where athletes can compete without concerns about sexual orientation. They offer a number of resource materials for coaches and athletes, including a workbook designed to provide guidance on how to create a sports environment where gays and lesbians will feel comfortable, secure and safe.

Summary

I have been in and around soccer for many years as a parent, coach, manager, teacher and player. In this time, I have come to fully understand the critical importance of "quality, standards, codes of conduct, responsibility and understanding." These are not simply words without meaning, but rather important ingredients that ensure everyone in the team fulfills their obligations toward a healthy, happy, safe and enjoyable experience within soccer. These ingredients must never be compromised, regardless of your role or involvement. As mentioned at the beginning of this chapter, a well-run club or school team can have an immensely positive impact on the social attitude and actions of those involved – perhaps even more so than school or the workplace. The environment you help to create is exciting, fun and caring, educational, inspiring and challenging – all things that help to positively shape a young person's movement through life.

As a teacher or coach, continually reflect on your role and the manner in which you deliver your education or coaching. As a parent, always consider the impact you are having on your child in the responses and advice you give them. Is it positive? Is it helpful? Is it relevant to the betterment of your child's development?

As a player, simply show respect for everything that is provided to you – the rides to games and training, the coaching given, the financial support and facilities provided. Finally, I urge all spectators to be fair, rational and respectful toward the officials, the players, the opposing team and the organizers. Enjoy the experience of watching the game and seeing the development of those involved. If all these ingredients can be blended correctly, the basic foundation is set for an enjoyable experience for everyone involved.

chapter 2
CHILD PROTECTION AND SAFETY

The majority of children who play sports do so in a safe and helpful atmosphere, with genuine support from coaches, volunteers and other club staff. But for the small minority of children who are abused during sporting activities, the picture is very different.

The sports community recognizes the need to protect children from individuals who might abuse positions of trust. In your work as a sports professional, there are a number of steps you can take to help safeguard children and young people. You can also play an important role in protecting children who may be experiencing abuse in other areas of their lives.

As discussed in Chapter 1 with regard to equality and fairness, it is vital that you develop a robust code of conduct to deal with issues of child protection, abuse and neglect. If your club receives any public funding, you are obliged to have such a policy in place.

I have detailed below some of the issues you must consider and include in this process. First, I have outlined definitions of abuse and neglect you should strive to prevent, and then discussed issues of staffing and facilities, and other considerations, that should constitute your club's policies and code of conduct.

Further information on child protection and safety issues discussed in this chapter can also be found at:

- www.soccer.org/Programs/SafeHaven
- www.childwelfare.gov
- www.canadasoccer.com
- www.protectchildren.ca

Child Abuse and Neglect

According to the Federal Child Abuse Prevention and Treatment Act and the Keeping Children and Families Safe Act, a "child" generally means any person under the age of 18. This raises issues of responsibility, self-awareness and a

---

Safe Haven

The American Youth Soccer Organization (AYSO) created the Safe Haven program to comply with the Child Protection Act and the Volunteer Protection Act. The child protection aspect of the program aims to stop child abuse, educate or remove its perpetrators, and screen out predators before they can become involved in youth soccer. With the understanding that children are more likely to be abused in a weak, unfocused or non-empowering environment, Safe Haven includes proactive steps that provide a medium for positive and healthy child development.

Because Safe Haven was the first program of its kind in American youth sports, AYSO offers assistance to other youth sports organizations interested in developing similar programs. Visit www.soccer.org/Programs/SafeHaven for more information.

---

young person's maturity. For example, a young person may feel ready to engage in sexual activity when they reach the legal age of consent, though they may still legally be a child. Therefore, some situations you could encounter might be less black and white than they first appear. Let's consider definitions of abuse and neglect, with some examples you might witness in practice.

Abuse

Child abuse can be defined as physical, emotional or sexual harm perpetrated by someone on a young person directly. Such examples might include:

- Physical bullying or maltreatment, including hitting and shaking, or forcing an individual to perform to an inappropriate level, e.g., making a young person do far too much physical exercise for their development.
- Inappropriate sexual behavior for the abuser's self-gratification, such as unwarranted physical contact with a young person, exposing them to pornography or making lewd remarks.
- Humiliation or unfair "singling-out" for criticism during sporting activity.

Neglect

Neglect is the systematic failure of those in authority to adequately account for a young person's psychological or physical needs, or failure to prevent them from coming to harm. Examples of neglect could include:

- Failing to provide sufficient warm clothing during activities on a cold day, or not allowing liquid refreshment on a hot day.
- Exposing a young person to undue risks of abuse or injury.
- Failing to act on signs of possible abuse by others.
- Not providing adequate access to other means of help and support for young people with problems.

Responsible Adults

In this section, we need to look at how to recruit and manage staff and volunteers, ensure they are well versed with rules and requirements, detail those requirements and also consider other factors where adults and young people come into contact in the course of their involvement at your club.

Staff and Volunteer Recruitment

It should go without saying that you must be extremely vigilant and thorough when it comes to interviewing and hiring staff and volunteers. It is important to note that any adult taking a role at your club must:

- have a clear role, be it a head coach, assistant coach or other
- have substantiated qualifications for the specific role
- if possible, provide references from previous employers/organizations
- have no criminal record
- sign up to your club's child protection policy in full

As we discussed in Chapter 1, children and young people are suggestible, so a good example must be set by anyone working at your club. This means that they should not use abusive, obscene or otherwise bad language, should not smoke or consume alcohol in the presence of young people in their care, or use drugs; nor should they encourage or glamorize any such habits. In turn, any responsible person at your club must not tolerate the above at any time, either by a young

Criminal Records Checks

Given the influential position they hold, it is vital that soccer clubs do thorough background checks on everyone who will be working with kids, be they an employee or a volunteer. A good place to start is the National Sex Offender Registry and your state's sex offender registry. The FBI's Crimes Against Children Unit coordinates the development and implementation of the National Sex Offenders Registry (NSOR), which tracks the whereabouts and movements of certain convicted sex offenders. The National Crime Information Center (NCIC) enables the NSOR to retain the offender's current registered address and dates of registration, conviction, and residence. Members of the public can check the NSOR by visiting www.nsopr.gov. States also maintain their own registries, and these should be consulted as well. A list of state registries can be found on the FBI's website at www.fbi.gov/hq/cid/cac/states.htm.

For a complete criminal records check consult your local and state police forces, as there is no centralized federal registry for criminal checks.

In Canada, in accordance with the Criminal Records Act, the process of obtaining criminal records checks of applicants for paid or volunteer work with "vulnerable persons" must begin at the local police service and not at a privately operating fingerprinting firm. Volunteer Canada, a national volunteerism organization, offers a wealth of information about screening volunteers on their website, www.volunteer.ca, including a brochure entitled "Understanding Police Records Checks" that can be downloaded directly from the site.

While Canada does have a National Sex Offender Registry, the public does not have access to it. Maintained by the RCMP in partnership with the provinces and territories, the National Sex Offender Registry gives police officers rapid access to current vital information on convicted sex offenders, such as addresses and telephone numbers, offences, aliases and identifying marks and tattoos.

While ensuring the safety of players is paramount, the information obtained during criminal checks should be used fairly. Someone applying to work with young people who has a conviction such as credit card fraud does not necessarily need that conviction made public by the club if it is irrelevant to the role. Only if that person were in a role that could involve misappropriation of club funds or the funds of a disabled child in their care might disclosure be deemed necessary. Even then, the information should be disseminated on a need-to-know basis only. Clubs should also ensure that all personal information is stored responsibly and, when the time comes, disposed of appropriately to ensure that confidentiality is maintained.

person or another adult. There can also be issues of a sexual nature to deal with. Something "innocent" may inadvertently become an inquiry; similarly, incidences of criminal behavior could occur unbeknown to you. The robustness of your code of conduct to deal with such matters will provide a clearly drawn line of acceptable and unacceptable behavior by anyone in your club.

Physical Contact and Sexual Abuse

Physical contact – between a responsible adult and a young person or between one young person and another – must only occur in the strict context of sports activity and/or skills improvement, or when administering first aid.

Positioning a child to demonstrate the correct way to conduct an exercise may involve physical contact from the adult teaching the skill. This should only occur in full view of other participating young people and only when necessary. The adult in question must explain the context of what they are doing both to the child and others present. There is never a reasonable excuse for touching a child's genital area, buttocks or breasts. When supervising disabled children, it must be decided before any activities take place what contact with the child is or is not acceptable with the child's parents/caregivers (and preferably the children themselves) and to gain strict permission.

In the case of injury to a child, any incidence must be officially recorded and parents informed of any treatment given, which may or may not have involved physical contact. As with demonstrating exercises, any contact must be in strict context, avoid sexually sensitive areas of the child's body and be explained to the child. Any incident where an adult inadvertently hurts a child – for example, a coach refereeing a practice game might run with the play and accidentally knock over a standing child they haven't seen in their path – must also be officially recorded and reported to parents. For more information on first aid and medical attention, see Chapter 3.

Any incident that occurs where a child reacts in a certain unexpected way or misinterprets an activity, where the adult in question's behavior is blameless, should also be officially reported and parents informed. An example of this could be a child's apparent sexual arousal by innocent physical contact.

The golden rule for physical contact is that if the young person can do something without you needing to touch them, there should be no contact. It's as simple as that.

Sexual contact

Any relationship or sexual contact between an adult over the age of 18 and young person under the age of 16 is regarded as a criminal act and should be treated as such by your club if it occurs. See later in the chapter for more information on dealing with this.

As I mentioned at the beginning of this chapter, lines can be blurred where a child under 18 but over the age of 16 is involved. Your policy must prohibit any relationship between a young person and anyone with a position of authority within your club, even if the young person is 16 or over. The conflict of such a personal relationship with the duty of care for young people in their jurisdiction makes such a position of authority untenable, especially considering the possible emotional immaturity of young people in their care.

For example, if a relationship involved a male coach and a teenage girl, she might feel obliged to partake in acts of a sexual nature she would otherwise not be happy to, in order to keep in favor with the coach in question. Also, if the coach has singled out this individual for such attention, she might feel special and therefore use this to misguidedly try to enhance her own status with her peers. For the coach's part, he might demonstrate favoritism that conflicts with the system of equal opportunity at your club, e.g., picking the girl for every game and not offering the same opportunities to play to other young people.

Among children themselves at your club, sexual relationships are quite likely to occur, just as they are at school or anywhere else where young people spend time together. Any outward behavior, even holding hands and kissing, etc., should be strongly discouraged during group activities and games, if only because it is unfair to other young people and can be discomfiting and distracting to them. Try pointing this out to individuals involved and ask, would they like it if someone else were doing it when they wanted to get on with an activity? In my experience, the answer always a firm "no"!

How to Act on Signs of Abuse

Both the Child Welfare Information Gateway (www.childwelfare.gov) in the United States and the Canadian Centre for Child Protection (www.protectchildren.ca) offer resources and advise on both how to recognize signs of abuse and help a victim of abuse.

Below is a simple checklist of what to do or provide at your club to effectively deal with signs of abuse:

- Ensure that there is a rigid framework in your code of conduct for recording and acting on allegations or signs of abuse (see sample record form on page 33).
- Take all allegations or signs of abuse extremely seriously.
- Listen carefully to everything a young person tells you, even if the details are hard for you to deal with, or if you find it a shock or difficult to believe at first hearing.
- Remember that young people are all different and will act and react differently in any given situation.
- Within context of allegations or signs of abuse, involve other responsible adults at your club with your investigations and reporting, e.g., if a girl alleging abuse feels more comfortable talking to a female member of your club staff, ensure that she has the opportunity to do so.
- Do not confront or involve in an inquiry any adult at your club that is the subject of allegations.
- Keep a lookout for any nonverbal signs of abuse, e.g., unusual bruising on a child's body or uncharacteristic behavior from a particular child that could hint at untoward activity.

On the Field

You must make staff aware of the need to be vigilant when supervising groups of young people, particularly if the field is public or in a publicly accessible area. Make sure that a list of children is always handy for a group so that you can keep tabs on which child is where. Younger children are naturally more demanding, easily distracted and naive, so a smaller child-to-adult ratio is needed for younger children.

Another useful system is "buddies," which is explained further in the "out and about" section later in this chapter.

If equipment is in use, you should check that children know how to use it properly and that it meets suitable standards of safety (see the section on risk assessments, pages 37–39). For example, ensure that goalposts are sufficiently anchored to the ground; do not let children hang from the crossbar of the goal, etc.

Other Adults

There will be times when there will be other adults, such as photographers or journalists, present at practices or games for perfectly legitimate reasons.

You must ensure that these reasons are definite, and that any visiting journalist or photographer is aware in advance of your club's code of conduct, health and safety issues and so on. If you are hiring them for their services, for example to use video footage for training purposes, you should check beforehand that the staff/company are reputable.

All photographing, videoing or interviewing (as appropriate) should be supervised, and no individual children should be separated from a group without the strictest appropriate context, and this certainly must not be done out of sight.

Consent forms must be completed and signed by a parent or guardian in advance of any photographing or filming that occurs, for every child appearing, and detailing the specific event in question, and forms officially kept. (See page 33 for a sample consent form.) Should any parent object, the child in question must not appear in any photography or filming. If this is unavoidable, the event must not be filmed.

Parents are naturally proud of their children – they will want to take photographs and, with video cameras so affordable and even cell phone technology

Sample Consent Form for the Use of Photographs or Video (Parents and Children)

(*Club or organization*) recognizes the need to ensure the welfare and safety of all young people in sports.

In accordance with our child protection policy we will not permit photographs, video or other images of young people to be taken without the consent of the parents/caregivers and children.

(*Club or organization*) will follow the guidance for the use of photographs, a copy of which is available from (*insert name*).

(*Club or organization*) will take all steps to ensure these images are used solely for the purposes they are intended. If you become aware that these images are being used inappropriately you should inform (*club or organization*) immediately.

I (*parent/caregiver*) consent to (*club or organization*) photographing or videotaping (*insert name*).

Date...

I (*name of child*) consent to (*club or organization*) photographing or videotaping my involvement in (*sport*).

Date...

now so readily available with cameras, in many cases wish to film their kids playing soccer. In these cases, parents should be given clear advice on when and how it is appropriate to gain this kind of footage. This can be included in your code of conduct for parents and children (see later in this chapter for more on this).

Out and About
Contact details

A child's registration with your club must include taking and carefully storing contact details. The first and obvious reason for this is in case of an emergency where an individual's parents need to be informed of an injury, for example.

The other reason is lateness. If you are at an away game and are delayed, policy should be in place to notify parents of any changes to plans or details at the earliest opportunity. Contact details should also contain a fallback" option in case the first point of contact is unavailable. This can be another relative of the child, or even parents of another friend within the same club/team.

Another excellent idea for disseminating changes of plan quickly and more easily for you is to set up a phone pyramid whereby you call two people, who call two more people and so on until everyone in the pyramid in descending order has been contacted. You should ensure that everyone in the list has given their full consent to be added and that the pyramid can be adapted at short notice in case of trouble contacting one of the principal names. For example, Mary Smith in the sample pyramid on page 35 could be unreachable for some reason, so contingencies must be in place to work around the pyramid differently to contact everyone.

Time changes

A key to this part of club policy is to publish clear times for regular training sessions and try to rigidly stick to these so that parents can plan when to collect their children. Where fixtures or times do have to change, you must let parents know at the earliest opportunity.

Another advantage of the contact details is in cases where a parent is unable to collect their child at the expected time. In these situations, you *must* contact the parent in question to explain the situation. Under no circumstances should you allow another parent to drive the child home instead, unless express permission has been given by the parent when you've contacted them for other arrangements to be made. Even then, this should only happen if they are known to the child and trusted by the parent. You should also not allow staff members (including yourself) to drive a young person home unless it is absolutely necessary and is the only option available. Even then, this should only be with the parent's prior consent. You should also never allow anyone to leave any young person in a vehicle unattended. Remember that you have a duty of care to a child until they are safely delivered back to their parents.

Other contacts:
Maria Gomes (Coach) – 555-8884
Darren Martyn (Coach) – 555-7891
Demarion Alexander (Chairman) – 555-6555

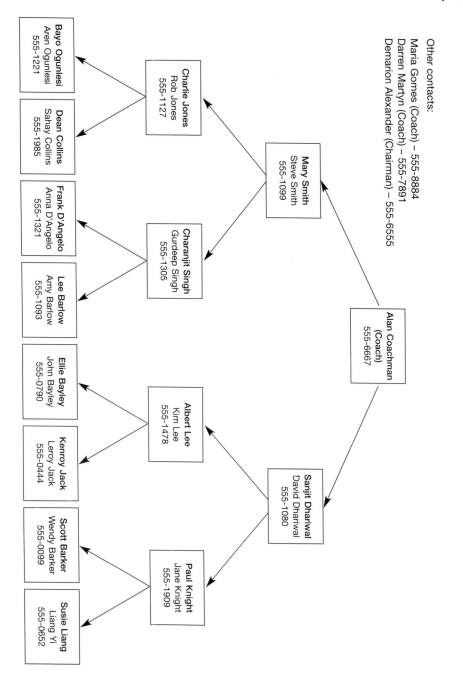

Bayo Ogunlesi
Aren Ogunlesi
555-1221

Dean Collins
Sahay Collins
555-1985

Charlie Jones
Rob Jones
555-1127

Frank D'Angelo
Anna D'Angelo
555-1321

Lee Barlow
Amy Barlow
555-1093

Charanjit Singh
Gurdeep Singh
555-1305

Mary Smith
Steve Smith
555-1099

Alan Coachman
(Coach)
555-6667

Ellie Bayley
John Bayley
555-0790

Kenroy Jack
Leroy Jack
555-0444

Albert Lee
Kim Lee
555-1478

Scott Barker
Wendy Barker
555-0099

Susie Liang
Liang Yi
555-0652

Paul Knight
Jane Knight
555-1909

Sanjit Dhariwal
David Dhariwal
555-1080

Transportation needs

You should take into account particular requirements of any young people in your care when on the road. For example, suitable vehicles/access may be required for some disabled individuals, or medicines looked after, e.g., asthma inhalers kept with the child.

Supervising groups of children

As we've already discussed, it is vitally important to know where all the children are in your care, and that they are safe. This can become even more difficult when you are in a strange town or away from your familiar home environment, particularly when you have a number of highly excited children to look after. Make sure that you have sufficient staff numbers to cope with this change of environment and that you are placed in such a way as to see all the children (for example, at opposite ends of a "crocodile" of children walking down the street). Disabled children should also be given adequate supervision according to their needs.

Another good system is "buddies" where each child has a partner, whom they seek out whenever you call out "Buddy!" Best friends will usually be with their buddy already, but more mobile children within the group will be able to seek theirs out elsewhere and confirm that all are present and correct. Where there is an uneven number, ensure that the odd number makes up a group of three with two buddies to find. If a disabled child is on the trip, even though they will be given extra supervision, do include them in the buddy system so that they are an inclusive part of the group.

Though this is a fun way of keeping tabs on numbers, and should be treated as such, you should also explain to children why the game is being played, and make sure that they don't suddenly decide to change buddies halfway through the trip!

In the Changing Rooms

You are likely to need changing facilities at your club. Separate provision must be made for male and female changing, supervised by two adults of the same gender as the young people concerned. Staff should not change or shower at the same time in the same facility as the children.

Young people can be sensitive about changing or undressing in front of their peers. If unhappy about doing so, they should not be forced to shower or undress in the changing rooms. In these situations, it is advisable to encourage the young person to shower as soon as they get home and to think about their personal hygiene in this way.

You should keep an eye out for any bullying or teasing directed at a young person when changing or showering, and take action to stop this happening in accordance with your code of conduct.

As with transport, it is necessary to ensure that disabled people have sufficient facilities. If a parent or caregiver is required to help with changing, the same gender rules apply as for staff. For example, a mother changing her son will need a changing room separate from other males. This should be handled sensitively so that the child does not feel too segregated.

Club Facilities – Health and Safety Risk Assessment

Your duty of care toward young people and issues of neglect extend to facilities and equipment. Regular risk assessments should be completed, using the same key criteria each time. An example of a completed risk assessment form is on pages 41–42; a blank form for you to use is in the appendices on pages 204–5. First, here are the criteria and sections you should include in detail.

1. The venue, date and name/position of person carrying out the assessment should be clearly marked. This person must be of some authority within your organization.
2. Check all areas that will be used for activities, such as hard-standing areas, fields, etc. Check for any obstacles or other hazards (litter, broken bottles, dog waste) or other factors likely to be a risk to safety. Make a note of any obstructions, hazards and action taken.
3. Any equipment, fixed or portable, must be looked at carefully. Goals are likely to be the most important of these, so:
   - check condition, i.e., for corrosion. Rust can weaken some metal structures, but more often it can cause overlying paint to peel, crack and/or expose bare metal that then corrodes further, with the risk of abrasion or laceration if contact is made.
   - check anchorage to ground. Weighting is important, no matter how large or heavy goal structures are, or if they are fixed or movable. Portable goals should be weighted with chain anchors when in use to prevent forward

movement or collapse, and locked up in a secure place/position when not in use to avoid unauthorized use/misuse. Larger, fixed goals should be anchored more securely, preferably into the ground. Check anchorage by exerting *reasonable* force forward, backward and sideways on the posts, and downward on the crossbar.

- ensure hooks for attaching nets to goals are made from plastic, so that they are flexible on contact. Metal cup hooks are dangerous and should be removed and/or replaced.
- check goals are as manufactured, not customized in some way that compromises safety, e.g., cut down to a smaller height.

Make a note of any offending items of equipment removed or replaced, or further action to take.

4. Are your players all registered fully with up-to-date emergency contact details? (See more on page 34.)

5. Check players all have the following, or have been briefed to bring it with them:
- running shoes or soft-studded soccer shoes (if playing indoors or on Astroturf)
- studded boots if playing on grass (running shoes are only acceptable if the ground is completely dry)
- shinpads. Many players don't consider it necessary to protect their shins, which are only one mistimed tackle away from being painfully skinned, bruised or even broken without shinpads. Even if the level of contact isn't as great as a full game, ensure that young people in your club get used to wearing shinpads at all times when practicing.
- a drink. While clubs and schools provide water bottles, these are more often than not passed around several players, contain old water from last week, and look pretty sorry besides, covered in mud from being tossed onto the ground during training, picking up germs from the ground. Encourage your players to bring a bottle – with their name on it, preferably – containing a non-carbonated drink for their own consumption. Make sure it's kept upright during the session, ideally in a carry-tray so it's away from the ground completely.
- a towel. Even if they cannot be persuaded to shower (see page 36), at least they can dry themselves off if it's been raining.

- a change of clothing. Even if the young person is wearing the correct gear, quite often they won't have brought anything dry or clean to change into afterward. Not only is sitting around in wet and dirty clothes not great for a child's health, it hardly helps their parents' car upholstery either. Encourage the wearing of a tracksuit so that it can be put back on after the game or practice. You might even want to get a club training uniform for all the kids to wear as well a playing uniform for the game itself.

6. Emergency access – is there sufficient access for emergency vehicles in the event of an accident? Any parked cars should be away from entrances from the road and to playing areas.

7. Ensure safety information, basic first aid advice (see also Chapter 3) and emergency telephone numbers are on display around the club. Note down what is/was missing and what action has been/will be taken.

8. Sign and print your name.

Other Help with Setting Up Child Protection Policy

As well as the American Youth Soccer Organization's Safe Haven program, other organizations are very active with child protection, and these can help you develop and implement your own policy.

Youth Soccer and Child Protection

The American Youth Soccer Organization (AYSO) was the first youth sports organization to create a formal program to comply with the Child Protection Act and the Volunteer Protection Act, and they offer assistance to other youth sports organizations interested in developing their own programs. These can be tailored to other organizational structures, even other sports. AYSO can be reached at www. soccer.org/Programs/SafeHaven or by calling (800) USA-AYSO.

Child Welfare Information Gateway

A service of the Children's Bureau, Administration for Children and Families, U.S. Department of Health and Human Services, the Child Welfare Information Gateway provides access to print and electronic publications, websites and online databases covering a wide range of topics from prevention to permanency, including child welfare and child abuse and neglect. The Child Welfare Information Gateway's website, www.childwelfare.gov, offers general information such as definitions of abuse and neglect, national and state statistics, characteristics of perpetrators (including those who commit certain types of abuse, such as juvenile sex offenders), definitions and signs of maltreatment types, research on child neglect, sexual abuse, physical abuse, emotional abuse and the risk factors that contribute to child abuse and neglect, including the characteristics of parents, caretakers, families, children and communities that increase risk.

Among the publications available to download from the website are detailed guides on how to create, implement, develop and maintain child abuse and neglect prevention programs. These include standards for prevention programs, research that demonstrates what works, types of prevention programs, reports from state programs and the roles of related professionals. Detailed information is also available on reporting cases of abuse or neglect, including how to report a suspected case of abuse, the systems that receive and respond to the reports and how the reports are investigated, assessed and managed.

Canadian Centre for Child Protection

The Canadian Centre for Child Protection is a nonprofit charitable organization dedicated to the personal safety of all children. Their goal is to reduce child victimization by providing programs and services to Canadians in three key areas: intervention, education and prevention. Recognizing that child sex offenders will often seek out opportunities to work and volunteer with children, the Canadian Centre for Child Protection is creating a child protection kit that outlines child protection policies, recruitment and screening standards, a mechanism for identifying and reporting potential abuse and a guide for parents. See www. protectchildren.ca for details.

Risk Assessment Form

Venue/Date: **Adams Park, Springfield – 18/08/07**
Name/position: **A. Coachman (Head Coach)**

Playing/Training Area

Are areas free of dangerous obstacles? Is area fit and appropriate for chosen activity? (Tick appropriate response.)

Yes   No   ✔

Outline any hazards and detail what action was taken or will be taken:

Debris and bottles left on field, now disposed of.

Goalposts/other equipment

Are goalposts safe and appropriate for the activity? Yes   No   ✔

Outline any unsafe equipment, who may be at risk and what action was taken:

Offending metal cup hook removed from crossbar and replaced with plastic net hook; sharp, rough rust patch on left-hand upright sanded down and repainted.

Players

Is the emergency contacts/medical register completed and up-to-date?

Yes   No   ✔

Outline current state and what action was taken:

Charanjit Singh's family moved to a new house last week, so Charanjit updated me with new address and his dad's new cell number for emergencies.

Is all the players' attire appropriate and safe for chosen activity?

Yes   No   ✔

Outline any unsafe equipment/attire and any action taken:

Kenroy Jack has lost his shinpads; found suitable replacements for now in equipment store and asked Kenroy to try and buy a new pair for next week.

Emergency Access

Can emergency vehicles access areas safely and without obstacle?

Neighboring house has permission to use the club parking lot, but owners have parked at the entranceway, so have asked them to park car in the parking lot itself.

Is telephone working?

Yes, tested it by calling my own cell number, which worked.

chapter 3
HEALTH AND WELFARE

First-aid

Did you know that by giving up just three hours one evening you could obtain a qualification in emergency first aid that might save a life? It is common sense for people to have some knowledge of first aid. Knowing the basics is invaluable and may be called upon in everyday life, not just when you are associated with soccer. So the obvious recommendation is, get qualified.

Taking a basic emergency first-aid course is simple. There is no test or written exam. You just need to demonstrate to the instructor that you have learned the techniques and can put them into practice. I can truly say that every first-aid course I have been on has been fun and enjoyable, and has given me the opportunity to make new friends. Each time I have learned new things and refreshed the areas I had forgotten. To get first-aid training, you can contact the organizations that run the courses (see boxes below and on page 44).

Red Cross

The Red Cross run a number of courses that will be relevant to working at your club. The 6-hour Basic First Aid/CPR/AED course is one of the Red Cross's most popular and is designed for community needs. It combines lectures, demonstrations, hands-on training and practice in subjects such as cardio-pulmonary resuscitation (CPR, see pages 49–50 for more details), automated external defibrillator (AED) training, shock, heat and cold emergencies, sudden illnesses, poisonings and first aid for everything from cuts and scrapes to muscle, bone and joint injuries.

The American Red Cross also teamed up with the United States Olympic Committee to design a Sport Safety Training Program specifically designed for coaches, athletic trainers and others interested in sports. The program aims to keep athletes safe, enable coaches and trainers to prevent, prepare for and respond to sports-related injuries, raise awareness of safety issues in athletics, and provide an atmosphere in which athletes can train and compete with a properly trained coach. The training focuses on helping coaches and athletic trainers identify and eliminate potentially hazardous conditions, recognize emergencies and make appropriate decisions for first-aid care. Options include a stand-alone Sports Injury Prevention and First Aid Course with additional training available in adult and child CPR and AED.

To find your local Red Cross and learn more about the courses they offer see www.redcross.org.

St. John Ambulance

Both the Red Cross and St. John Ambulance run first-aid courses in Canada. The Red Cross's Standard First Aid and CPR course is similar to the Basic course offered in the U.S., including AED certification. See www.redcross.ca for more details.

The relevant course run by the St. John Ambulance is the Standard Level First Aid course, which covers five core areas – cardiovascular emergencies and CPR, emergency-scene management, choking, severe bleeding and shock, unconsciousness and fainting – and 18 electives that include medical conditions such as diabetes and asthma, child resuscitation, AED, bone and joint injuries, head/spinal and pelvic injuries, chest injuries, heat and cold illness and injuries, wound care and multiple casualty management. See www.sja.ca for details.

It is important that coaches are qualified in all aspects of dealing with young people. These days, coaching certificates at all levels incorporate child protection workshops and first aid. Additionally, coaches should ensure they have appropriate professional and public liability insurance. It is common sense that you are adequately insured against any claims of negligence that might be made.

At my local club we also ensure that at least one other regular attendee at the games – such as an assistant manager or parent – is qualified in first aid and child protection. To encourage participation, the club even pays for them to take the courses. The number of people at our club qualified in first aid is growing, from senior-level players to parents and officials. It should not be difficult to get people at your club to attend a first-aid or child protection course. Common sense says they should attend.

The bottom line is you never know when you are going to need your emergency first-aid skills. In a sport like soccer where there is a high probability of injury, knowing basic emergency first-aid procedures could prevent a serious injury from getting worse and even save a life!

Keeping a Record

If an injury or incident occurs, you must make an official record and inform the child's parents, even if the child is fit enough to continue an activity after treatment.

First-aid Procedures: Basic Conditions and Treatments

As I've said, there is no substitute for a professional first-aid course, but as a handy reference to photocopy and take onto the field with you, the following pages contain the most common problems and conditions you might have to deal with. You should always be well prepared, so ensure that you keep a comprehensive first-aid kit on the sidelines at all times in case of emergency (see box below). And if you use any of the contents – make sure you replace them!

Equipment for the First-aid Kit

- Small waterproof zip bag
- Protective disposable gloves (latex)
- Sterile gauze squares
- Disposable bag for gloves, gauze squares, etc.
- Butterfly skin closures
- Small spray bottle containing sterile water for wound cleansing
- Disposable ice pack
- 3-inch (7.5 cm) elastic adhesive bandage to hold gauze pad(s) in position
- Roll of 1-inch (2.5 cm) zinc oxide tape for gauze fixation in cases of bleeding
- Bandages (various sizes)
- Two large sterile roller bandages for profuse bleeding

The primary survey (DRAB/C)

Danger

Before you assess the casualty, make sure that neither you nor the casualty is in danger. In most cases, the game or activity will stop immediately so that this can be done safely.

Response

If the casualty has been knocked out or appears unconscious, check by shouting something like, "Can you hear me?" and shake them gently by the shoulders if necessary. Is there a response?

- **Yes** – summon help onto the field or activity area as required, but do not move the casualty. Treat any condition that has arisen and monitor pulse and breathing continually until further medical assistance arrives.
- **No** – immediately call for help. If the casualty is on their back, open their airway. If they are in a different position and it is unavoidable, turn them gently onto their back and then open the airway.

Airway

Place one hand on the casualty's forehead and tilt the head back. Use two fingers of the other hand to lift the chin, so that the tongue is moved away from the back of the mouth (see below).

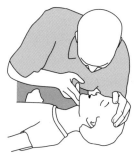

Breathing/CPR

Look to see if the casualty's chest is rising and falling; place your head close to the mouth to listen for breathing or to sense the heat of the casualty's breath on your own skin (see illustration below). Are they breathing normally?

- **Yes** – place them in the recovery position (see page 48).
- **No** – you should begin cardiopulmonary resuscitation (CPR; see more on pages 49–50); if the casualty is breathing but not in a normal or regular way, you should still begin CPR. (For example, the condition *agonal breathing* can occur after a sudden cardiac arrest, resulting in sudden irregular gasps.)

Note

Historically, the C in DRAB/C stood for *Circulation*, but in some revised modern protocols, this step stands for *Cardiopulmonary resuscitation* or, more simply, *Compressions*, which is effectively artificial circulation.

Once oxygen can be delivered to the lungs by a clear airway and efficient breathing, there needs to be a circulation to deliver oxygen to the rest of the body. This can be initially assessed in a number of ways, including a pulse check, breath being inhaled/exhaled, rising and lowering of the chest, pale skin showing color returning, and a warming up of the body temperature.

The recovery position

A casualty should only be placed in the recovery position if they are breathing normally:

- Turn the casualty onto their side.
- With the head to one side, tilt the chin forward to open the airway. Rest the casualty's cheek on their hand if necessary. If you suspect the casualty has a spinal injury, *do not* tilt the chin. Instead, place your hands on either side of their face, using your fingertips to lift the jaw gently and open the airway. This is known as the jaw thrust technique.
- Ensure that the casualty is positioned so that they cannot roll forward or backward.
- Keep a close eye on their vital signs (i.e., pulse and breathing) to make sure their condition is not deteriorating.
- Depending on the nature of their injuries, turn the casualty over to the other side after 30 minutes.

Cardiopulmonary resuscitation (CPR)

In the unlikely event that there is no one else present to call 911, you should give one minute of CPR to the casualty *before* calling 911 *if they are prepubescent.* With older children who have reached puberty, call the emergency services first and then administer CPR. If you are unsure, for the reasons discussed in the section in Chapter 2 on physical contact, it is inappropriate and unnecessary to check. In such cases, proceed with the adult version of CPR detailed below.

Children (up to puberty)

First, administer *rescue breaths:*

- Make sure that the airway is opened as described on page 46 for "Response."
- Pinch the nose and seal your lips around the child's mouth.
- Looking along the chest to see that the chest rises, blow gently into the lungs, ensuring that you do not completely empty your lungs.
- When the chest has risen, stop blowing and allow it to fall.
- Repeat four times (so, five rescue breaths in all), then check for circulation.

Then, administer *chest compressions:*

- Depending on the size/age of the child, place one or two hands in the center of the chest. It should be possible to determine the correct place without removing any of the child's clothing.
- Keeping your arms straight, use the heel(s) of your hand(s) to depress the chest one-third of its depth, and then release, leaving the hand(s) in position after the compression.
- Press 30 times at a rate of 100 compressions a minute (so a series of compressions should take 18 seconds), then give two rescue breaths as described above.

Continue the pattern of 30 compressions/two rescue breaths, without breaking the sequence, until further assistance arrives.

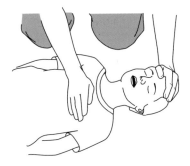

Older children/adults

First, administer *chest compressions*:

- Place the heel of one hand in the center of the chest. Place the other over the top of it and interlock the fingers of both hands.
- Keeping your arms straight and your fingers away from the chest, depress the chest by $1^{1}/_{2}$–2 inches (4–5 cm), then release, leaving the hands in position after the compression.
- Press 30 times at a rate of 100 compressions a minute (so a series of compressions should take 18 seconds).

Then, give two *rescue breaths* as described for younger children, above. Continue the pattern of 30 compressions/two rescue breaths, without breaking the sequence, until further assistance arrives.

Choking

There are two forms of choking, mild or severe, depending on the kind of obstruction. The instructions below relate to treatment of both children and adults so should cover all ages of young people you may have to treat.

Mild obstruction

The casualty will be conscious and breathing, and may be able to cough, and communicate distress through crying or speaking. It may be that they are eating or drinking too fast, or at an inappropriate time, e.g., when they are actually performing an activity.

Look immediately in the mouth for obvious objects causing obstruction and remove them. Encourage the young person to keep coughing to clear the obstruction, and keep them calm in case they panic and cause themselves harm. Keep monitoring the casualty to ensure their symptoms do not worsen.

Severe obstruction

In this case, the casualty will not be able to breathe, cough, cry or speak. If left unassisted, they will eventually become unconscious.

First, administer up to five *back blows* – quick, sharp blows between the shoulder blades with the heel of your hand. Immediately check the mouth and remove any obvious obstructions.

If the obstruction has not been cleared, give up to five *abdominal thrusts*. To perform abdominal thrusts (also known as the *Heimlich maneuver*), stand behind the casualty and wrap your arms around their middle. Holding one wrist with the other hand, place the clenched fist of the other hand between the navel and the bottom of the breastbone, and pull inward and upward. Check the mouth quickly after each thrust.

If the obstruction does not clear after three cycles of back blows and abdominal thrusts, call for an ambulance. Continue the cycle of blows and thrusts until help arrives or you have removed the obstruction. If you successfully remove the obstruction and the casualty is unconscious but breathing normally, place them in the recovery position (see page 48).

Limb fractures

There's a fair chance, with the rough and tumble of soccer activities and young people with growing bones, that fractures will occur. While you cannot actually treat the fracture itself, there are other things you can do to assist and calm the casualty:

- Keep the young person calm and reassure them that they will be OK.
- Persuade them to stay still, and do not move them yourself unless strictly necessary.
- Support the limb with your hands to prevent any movement that will cause more damage and/or distress.
- If there is bleeding, carefully press a clean pad over the wound to control the flow of blood. When you have done so, bandage carefully around the wound.
- If you suspect a broken arm, improvise a sling to support the arm close to the body (for guidance on how to make a sling, see the box below).
- If you suspect a broken leg, it is important to try and immobilize the leg by placing a pad between the knees and ankles, then gently but firmly bandaging the injured leg to the uninjured one, improvising a splint.
- Call for an ambulance.
- Continue to reassure the casualty and watch out for signs of shock (see page 61). If the casualty becomes unconscious, use the DRAB/C sequence and/or recovery position (see pages 46–48).
- Do not give the casualty anything to eat or drink in case they need an urgent operation on the fracture.

Making a Sling

Note: This advice does not replace proper first-aid training – there are various ways of making an emergency sling such as this; great caution should be exercised.

- Take a clean square bandage. Your first-aid kit should have one specifically for this purpose. Fold diagonally into a triangle.

- Slip the bandage underneath the arm (see illustration A below) so that one corner is at the neck and opposite shoulder from the arm to be slung.

- Bring the lower part up so that it cradles the arm in a secure position as close to the body as comfortably possible. Be careful not to cause pain and distress to the casualty when elevating the arm (see illustration B).

- Bring the second corner up to the neck on the same side of the arm and fasten carefully to the other side of the sling behind the neck with safety pins (illustration C).

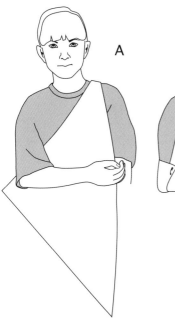
A

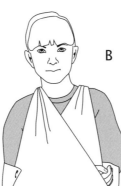
B

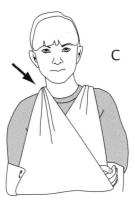
C

Bleeding

The most likely cause of bleeding in young people in your care will be through a cut, graze or scratch, e.g., from falling onto a hard playing surface or colliding with another player. Occasionally, a more serious injury may cause severe bleeding that you will need to contain until hospital treatment can be provided.

Minor bleeding

- Hygiene is essential. Wash your hands thoroughly and dry them. Cover any cuts, grazes or scratches on your own hands, and wear disposable gloves – these are as much to protect you from infection as the casualty.
- If dirt is in a cut, place it under running water (if possible). Pat dry with a sterile dressing or other clean lint-free material. If there is a foreign object lodged in the cut, you will need to follow a different procedure (see box below).

Objects in Wounds

If a large object is embedded in a cut that cannot be removed by washing with clean water, proceed as follows:

- Leave the foreign object in place.
- Apply firm pressure either side of the object.
- Raise and support the wounded limb or part, being careful not to cause undue pain or distress to the casualty.
- Lay the casualty down in case of shock (see more on shock on page 61).
- Gently cover the wound and the object with a sterile dressing.
- Build up layers of padding around the object until the level of padding is higher than the object, so that you can cover the object without placing pressure on it.
- Bandage over the object.
- If bleeding is light, seek medical attention at an emergency department or walk-inclinic for further treatment; if bleeding is severe, call an ambulance and treat the casualty for shock.

- Cover the wound temporarily with a sterile dressing or other clean lint-free material, then clean the area around the wound with soap and water, patting dry carefully with another clean material.
- Cover the wound completely with a sterile dressing or adhesive bandage.

Severe bleeding

- Again, wash your hands thoroughly and dry them. Cover any cuts, grazes or scratches on your own hands, and wear disposable gloves.
- To stem the bleeding, apply direct pressure to the wound with a pad (e.g., a clean lint-free cloth) or fingers until a sterile dressing is available.
- Lay the casualty down in case of shock (see more on shock on page 61).
- Raise and support the wounded limb or part, being careful not to cause undue pain or distress to the casualty.
- Bandage the pad or dressing firmly so as to staunch the flow of blood, but be careful not to bandage legs or arms too tightly and cut off circulation to the toes or fingers.
- If blood seeps through the bandage, do not remove it — apply another one over the top. If the blood continues to seep through the second bandage, only then should you remove the bandages and go through the process again.
- Call for an ambulance.
- Treat for shock (see page 61).

Nosebleeds

Nosebleeds are usually caused by rupturing of the tiny blood vessels in the nostrils. There are a number of ways that nosebleeds can occur during soccer activities – an impact on the nose from a ball at close range, or blowing the nose and sneezing (both common during allergy season), for example.

Some young people will be more predisposed to nosebleeds than others, so you should make a note of any child who is particularly susceptible. If the nosebleed is heavy, it can cause a dangerous loss of blood for the young person. Should this occur, follow the below procedures, but transport or send the child to the emergency department according to club rules (see Chapter 2, pages 37–8, for details on conduct when transporting children).

Note: If a heavy impact to the head causes a nosebleed where the blood is thin and watery, it is highly likely that the skull is fractured and fluid is leaking from around the brain. (For more on skull fractures, see page 58.)

- Sit the casualty down and ask them to tilt their head slightly forward, so that the blood will drain from their nostrils.
- Ask the casualty to pinch the soft part of their nose and keep it pinched, breathing through their mouth instead (which will also have a calming effect). *Do not* tilt the head back, as blood may run down the throat and induce vomiting or choking. Make sure the casualty does not cough, swallow, spit or especially sniff, as this may disturb blood clots forming in the nose.
- After 10 minutes, ask the casualty to stop pinching their nose but keep their head forward. If blood continues to flow, repeat the procedure for a further two periods of 10 minutes. If the bleeding continues after 30 minutes, transport or send the child to the emergency department according to club rules (see Chapter 2, pages 37–8, for details on conduct when transporting children). Ensure the child maintains the head-forward position in transit.
- If the bleeding has stopped, clean gently around the nose with clean, lukewarm water. Should the bleeding restart, begin process of treatment again.
- Tell the casualty to rest quietly for a few hours and not take part in any activities that might cause the blood clots in the nose to be disturbed.

Concussion

Concussion is caused by a blow to the head where the brain, which has some room to move within the skull, is shaken. There follows a brief period of impaired consciousness where some function is lost, usually only a few minutes – a classic example of this is a boxing match where a fighter is knocked out. can barely stand and seems confused about where they are and what is going on, but in fact is then sufficiently sound of mind to give a press interview shortly afterward. Concussion is very common in contact sports in general.

Recovery is usually complete, but some other symptoms may occur post-recovery, such as:

- mild, generalized headache
- dizziness and nausea
- no memory of event that caused concussion or events immediately after it.

If recovery is quick, ensure that they continue to rest, and make sure someone monitors their pulse, breathing and level of response to ensure that they do not deteriorate, indicating a worse head injury (see also information on skull fractures on page 58 and cerebral compression on page 60). If symptoms continue or worsen, or if any other symptoms occur, such as blurred vision or excessive sleepiness, seek medical attention.

Skull fracture

This injury hit the headlines in 2006 when goalkeeper Petr Cech of Chelsea collided head first with the boot of Reading's Stephen Hunt in an English Premiership game. Great concern was shown at the time of the injury, and Cech's rapid recovery (albeit to play in a rugby-style protective cap) surprised many experts.

There are few more serious injuries you will ever have to face than a skull fracture. Any head wound or injury should quickly be assessed to see if a possible fracture has occurred. Signs to look out for are:

- wound or bruise on the head
- soft area or depression on the scalp
- clear fluid or watery blood emerging from either ear and/or the nose
- blood in the white of the eye; bruising around either or both eyes
- distortion or lack of symmetry in the head or face
- impaired consciousness; progressive deterioration in level of response.

Remember that your job in this case is to ensure that the casualty is breathing and stable so that an ambulance can be called and emergency treatment sought. There are two possible courses of action to take, depending on the condition of the casualty.

Conscious casualty

- Help the casualty lie down.
- Make sure you *do not* turn the neck in case of a spinal/neck injury.
- Control any bleeding of the scalp by applying careful pressure around the wound (see pages 54–56 for more on treating bleeding).
- Call an ambulance.
- If there is discharge from the ear, place a clean pad or sterile dressing over the ear and lightly secure it with a bandage. Do not plug the ear.
- Keep a close eye on the casualty's breathing, pulse and their level of response (i.e., keep them talking) until the ambulance arrives.

Log-roll Technique

This technique is so named because it involves a number of people all rolling the casualty carefully and in a controlled manner at the same time like a log.

All working together, the team of people slowly turn the casualty over simultaneously, avoiding any bending, twisting or other movement that might further damage the spine or neck and cause paralysis.

Unconscious casualty

- Open the airway using the jaw-thrust technique and establish vital signs using the primary survey techniques described on pages 46–48, then follow the DRAB/C process as necessary.
- Call an ambulance.
- If the casualty is in a position that makes the jaw thrust impossible or an open airway difficult to maintain, and if you have assistance on hand, use the log-roll technique (see box above) to get the casualty into the recovery position.

Cerebral compression

This injury generally occurs when an impact to the head leads to pressure on the brain, with damaged brain tissue swelling or blood from the brain causing pressure within the skull. It is extremely serious and is most likely to occur in the same situations as a fractured skull (see page 58). However, unlike a fractured skull, the symptoms or effects of cerebral compression are not obvious immediately and can occur hours or even days later.

As with a skull fracture, the conscious casualty will display a deteriorating level of response, which could be accompanied by a change in personality/behavior such as irritability or disorientation, and may then fall unconscious. Other signs to look out for *in conjunction with the lack of response* are:

- slow, labored breathing
- slow but strong pulse
- unequal pupil size in eyes
- high temperature/flushed face
- weakness and/or paralysis down one side of the face or body.

If you are aware that one of the young people in your club has had a blow to the head for any reason in recent days (whether or not it was playing soccer), you may want to consider if it is sensible for the child to participate in any risky activity where a worse injury may occur.

Your first action should be to call an ambulance. Then treatment should be as follows:

Conscious casualty

- Make sure they are in a comfortable position, preferably with the minimum of movement, and reassure them.
- Monitor and record their level of response, pulse and breathing at regular intervals until the ambulance arrives.

Unconscious casualty

- Open the airway using the jaw-thrust technique and establish vital signs using the primary survey techniques described on pages 46–7, then follow the DRAB/C process as necessary.

Try to maintain an open airway with the casualty in the position they were found, even if that makes the jaw thrust difficult to perform.

Shock

Shock can occur as a result of serious injury and is usually due either to blood loss from an injury preventing vital organs (including the brain) from functioning properly or the body's reaction to psychological upset from fear or pain. Shock will almost always occur to a greater or lesser degree, but the symptoms may be missed if other obvious injuries are being attended to. Shock may also occur as a delayed reaction, hours afterward in some cases, so you should remain vigilant when treating a casualty. You should watch out for:

- pallid complexion or cold, clammy skin
- rapid, weak pulse
- quick, shallow breathing
- feeling sick or actual vomiting
- yawning or sighing.

In extreme cases, the casualty may fall unconscious. In this instance, you should place them in the recovery position and monitor them closely (see page 48 for more on the recovery position). If the casualty remains conscious, you should treat as follows:

- Give plenty of comfort and reassurance.
- Lay the casualty down, raising and supporting their legs so that blood will flow to vital organs (see illustration below).
- Do not allow the casualty to get too hot or cold. Use a blanket or coat to keep them warm, but do not smother them.
- Refrain from giving them food or drink, even if they ask for it.
- Regularly check the casualty's breathing and pulse. If they stop breathing, follow the DRAB/C process (see pages 46–7).
- If the casualty complains of difficulty breathing or begins to vomit, place them in the recovery position (see page 48).

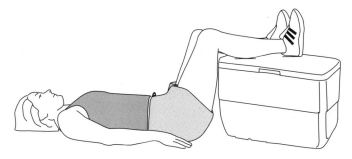

Heat exhaustion

The chances are that you'll be supervising activities at your club in the summer months, particularly during the summer holidays when kids are out all day long in strong sunshine. You should therefore be aware of the risks of heat exhaustion, heatstroke (see page 63) and sunburn (see page 64), as the effects can be debilitating and dangerous.

The main cause of any heat exhaustion you encounter is likely to be dehydration. Excessive sweating on hot days can leave the body short of the water it needs to function. Despite the regular reminders we hear of the danger of excessive salt intake, it should be remembered that salt in the right quantities is essential to organ function. The loss of salt through sweating is also a factor in heat exhaustion.

Symptoms to look out for are:

- headache
- pallid complexion or cold, clammy/sweaty skin
- rapid, weak pulse
- quick, shallow breathing
- dizziness/confusion
- feeling sick or actual vomiting
- loss of appetite
- muscle cramps in the abdominal wall, arms or legs.

You need to cool the casualty down and replenish their bodily fluids before any dangerous deterioration takes place in their condition. Treat as follows:

- Help the casualty if necessary to a cool place out of the sun.
- Lay the casualty down, raising and supporting their legs so that blood will flow to vital organs.
- Give the casualty plenty of water but discourage a large intake at once to avoid bloating which may cause vomiting.
- Give the casualty a weak salt solution, mixing one teaspoon of salt with a quart of water. Again, do not let the casualty drink this too suddenly in case of a nauseous reaction. Provide plenty of encouragement and assistance if necessary, as younger children in particular will probably find drinking the solution unpleasant.

- If the casualty's responses continue to deteriorate, place them in the recovery position (see page 48) and call an ambulance. Monitor vital signs and be prepared to give CPR if necessary (see pages 49–50).
- Even if the casualty makes a quick recovery, encourage them to seek medical attention in case of a relapse or any other ill effects.

Heatstroke

This condition is seen when the body's ability to regulate temperature (by the thermostat in the brain) is adversely affected. This can be caused by overexposure to the sun on hot days or as a result of the effects of heat exhaustion (see page 62). The body becomes dangerously overheated and functions can begin to fail. Note: Though there may be a causal link, heatstroke should not be confused with heat exhaustion, as some of the symptoms are different.

Symptoms to look out for are:

- headache
- hot, flushed/dry skin
- a full, bounding pulse
- dizziness/confusion/discomfort/restlessness
- a rapid deterioration in the level of response
- body temperature over 104°F (40°C).

You need to cool the casualty down before any further deterioration takes place in their condition. Treat as follows:

- Move the casualty as fast as possible to a cool place and remove as much of their outer clothing as possible (see page 29 in Chapter 2 for guidelines on appropriate contact with young people in doing this).
- Call an ambulance.
- Wrap the casualty in a cold, wet sheet or, if no sheet is available, fan them and sponge them with cold water. Continue to do this until their temperature drops to 100°F (38°C), then wrap them in a dry sheet or some other clean material, as available.
- Keep monitoring their vital signs until the ambulance arrives. If their temperature begins to increase again, repeat the cooling process, as above.

- If the casualty becomes unconscious, use the DRAB/C sequence (see pages 46–7) and be prepared to use CPR (see pages 49–50). If the casualty is unconscious but breathing normally, put them in the recovery position (see page 48) and monitor their breathing closely until the ambulance arrives.

Sunburn

Overexposure to sunlight is commonplace, particularly when the weather suddenly changes from rain to shine and cold snap to heatwave, leaving people unprepared. There is also still a certain degree of laissez-faire and ignorance among some people about the real dangers of prolonged sun exposure, fueled in part by the body-beautiful images of tanned celebrities seen in magazines and on TV.

You should make young people and their parents aware that they should be protecting themselves from sunburn, and/or making such provision available at your club. For times where children are outside for long periods, a high sun protection factor (SPF) sunblock is essential. If the ultraviolet (UV) index is high enough in summer to cause sunburn after only one hour, a low-SPF sunscreen may not be enough if the young person is out all day in the sun. It should also be remembered that even thin, high clouds let through enough ultraviolet light from the sun to cause sunburn, not just direct sunlight.

As well as sunscreen, encourage young people to wear a hat if possible, as this will protect their scalp, neck and face from increased exposure. It will also reduce the risk of heatstroke (see page 63).

Symptoms of sunburn are:

- reddened skin, often made more obvious by tan lines seen when clothing is changed or a white mark, e.g., a patch of pale skin revealed when the young person removes their watch
- stinging, soreness or burning pain of affected area
- blistering of the affected skin in severe cases (may occur a while after exposure).

Treatment is as follows:

- First and foremost, get the young person out of the sun, preferably indoors.
- In minor cases, cover the affected areas with thin clothing or a towel.
- Cool the skin by sponging, bathing or asking the casualty to take a 10-minute shower with cool water.

- Encourage the casualty to take regular sips of cold water.
- If necessary on minor sunburn, apply – or ask the casualty to apply as appropriate – after-sun cream or calamine lotion to the affected area.
- If the burns are severe and/or blistering occurs, seek medical advice or attention.
- Keep an eye out for symptoms of heatstroke that may result from prolonged exposure (see page 63).

Hypothermia

Hypothermia is a condition arising when the body cannot keep its core temperature high enough to function properly. Severe cases are unlikely to occur at your club, but the early stages of hypothermia might occur if you are outside on particularly cold days, especially if the weather is also inclement and/or windy. You should ensure that young people in your care wear sufficient clothing for the temperature and conditions (e.g., rain) and have sufficient fuel (i.e. food) to keep them going. More layers of thin clothing are better than fewer thick layers, as they trap more air for better insulation. Hats are also a good idea, as around 20 percent of body heat loss is through the head. And keep them moving, as exercise generates heat!

Symptoms to look out for in mild to moderate cases of hypothermia are:

- pronounced goose bumps on the skin
- bouts of shivering, becoming more violent as condition worsens
- grogginess/confusion
- lack of concentration or deterioration in level of response
- slow, shallow breathing
- slow, weak pulse.

If severe hypothermia sets in, shivering stops, irrational behavior such as stripping off layers of clothing may occur, and eventually the casualty will fall unconscious, but you will have spotted the danger signs and acted before it could ever get to this stage! To prevent severe hypothermia:

- Take the young person out of the cold/wind/rain.
- Put them in dry clothing if wet and add more thin layers to help warming – the main torso/trunk area is most important as this is where the core temperature is maintained.

- Give them a hot drink and something to eat, preferably also hot. Do not be tempted to give any young person a "medicinal" brandy or other warming alcoholic drink. No one of any age should be given alcohol to try to counter the effects of cold, as alcohol causes dilation of peripheral blood vessels, increasing heat loss.
- Do not wash hands or feet under hot water to warm them as this is likely to cause blistering and chilblains.
- Make sure the young person is supervised to ensure that their condition does not worsen.

Insect stings

On summer days, the air is usually thick with insects. When it comes to stings on days like this, most you are likely to experience will be from wasps. Most people dislike wasps, and many will panic or lash out in fear if they encounter one. Unfortunately, wasps are quite persistent when they pick up the scent of sweaty bodies and can react to flapping arms and swatting, which is when stings can occur. Less commonly, bees or hornets may also sting.

Your responsibility is to treat the sting with a minimum of fuss and arrange any medical treatment. You should also keep an eye out for any severe allergic reaction to the sting – known as anaphylaxis (see page 68), which is rare but can be fatal. The visual signs of the sting will be:

- swelling at site of sting
- redness around the sting.

To treat the casualty:

- Reassure the casualty and calm them down as much as possible. Younger children will probably be more distressed through the sheer unfamiliar pain of the sting.
- If the stinger is visible, brush or scrape it off the skin. To avoid stinging yourself, use the blunt side of a knife or a credit card to do this. Don't use tweezers or any other implement which may squeeze more poison from the stinger into the body or push the stinger further in
- Place ice or a cold pack on the sting to bring the swelling down and soothe the pain, if possible raising and supporting the affected part.

■ Monitor very closely any stings in and around the mouth (or even throat), as swelling can restrict the airway or even block it. In this case, try and give the casualty an ice cube to suck, or cold water to sip, that will reduce swelling. If breathing does become difficult, seek medical attention immediately.

■ If breathing is impaired and the sting is not in the mouth or throat, this may be as a result of allergic reaction. Other symptoms of allergy are swelling to the face, neck, tongue, mouth or lips (usually unconnected to the sting site), or widespread rash. An ambulance should be called immediately. See following page for more on anaphylaxis.

Severe allergic reaction – anaphylaxis

Fortunately, anaphylactic reactions are rare, but onset is sudden and can be fatal. The most likely causes you will encounter are allergic reactions to stings or reactions from the accidental consumption of nuts in young people who have nut allergies.

Symptoms of anaphylaxis are:

- impaired breathing, ranging from a tight chest to severe difficulty breathing, or wheezing/gasping for air
- swelling to the face, neck, tongue, mouth or lips, or widespread rash
- puffiness around the eyes
- anxiety
- signs of shock (see also page 61).

You should immediately call an ambulance, giving as much detail as possible on the likely cause of the allergic reaction and symptoms. If the casualty has any medication for the allergy, ask them to take it, or help them administer it if necessary. Then treat as follows:

Conscious casualty

- Help them sit up in a position that eases their breathing, usually leaning forward slightly.

Unconscious casualty

- If the casualty becomes unconscious and is not breathing sufficiently normally, follow the DRAB/C procedure (see pages 46–7).
- If they are unconscious but breathing as normally as possible in the circumstances, place in the recovery position (see page 48) until the ambulance arrives.

Asthma

Asthma is on the increase in young people, experts citing urban living and other lifestyle factors as a possible cause. The chances are that you will have one person, if not more, in your club with the condition. Air passages in the lungs spasm and linings of the airways swell, narrowing them and making breathing difficult. Likely triggers when you are supervising young people will be exercise, an allergic reaction (e.g., hay fever), a cold, or reaction to extremes of weather (e.g., a very cold or very hot day).

The chances are that anyone having an asthma attack will recognize their own symptoms, and will probably be able to deal with them in an assured manner. Usually, those who experience regular attacks carry a blue inhaler (e.g., salbutamol), which they can use unassisted, and maybe a spacer (plastic bottle-style attachment that acts to deliver the metered dose of inhalant more effectively). However, you should be aware of the symptoms should you have to step in and assist:

- the casualty will be having difficulty breathing, with a particularly long outward breath, which may also be wheezing
- a cough
- hypoxia – a lack of oxygen in the blood – which may produce a gray/blue tinge to the lips, ears and fingernail beds caused by the deoxygenated hemoglobin.

However, younger children may need help using their inhaler, or may be generally panicked or distressed. You should assist treatment as follows:

- Reassure the casualty and keep them calm.
- Encourage them to use their inhaler/spacer, assisting if necessary.
- Seat the casualty in a position where they can breathe the most easily – this is usually leaning forward with arms resting on the table or the back of a chair — and encourage them to breathe slowly and deeply. Do not lay them down.
- If the attack has not eased after three minutes, ask the casualty to use their inhaler again. If their condition deteriorates, seek medical assistance.

Note: If you are away from home and have young people with asthma in your care, ensure that they have sufficient inhaler medication with them for the time they are away, and that it is readily accessible should an attack occur (i.e., with the child on the bus and not stored in their luggage). For more on traveling with young people, see Chapter 2, page 34.

Hypoglycemia (low blood sugar)

The chances are that you will only experience a casualty with hypoglycemia if they are a diabetic, in which case they may, as with someone having an asthma attack, recognize the onset of a hypoglycemic episode. It can also occur as a result of heat exhaustion (see page 62) or hypothermia (see page 65).

Symptoms to look out for are:

- deteriorating rate of response, and/or strange, confused or aggressive behavior and actions
- weakness, faintness or hunger
- palpitations and muscle tremors
- sweaty and/or clammy, cold skin.

Conscious casualty

Your main objective for a conscious casualty is to raise blood-sugar levels as fast as possible to prevent further deterioration and unconsciousness:

- Help the casualty to sit or lie down.
- If they are a diabetic with their own glucose gel, help them administer it.
- In the absence of glucose gel, give them a sugary drink (make sure they are not Diet or Light drinks as these are sugar-free), chocolate or any other sweet food on hand. You should only do this if the casualty is *fully conscious* and able to swallow food or drink without choking.
- If the casualty recovers quickly, ask them to consume more food/drink, and rest. Advise their parents to take them to the doctor.
- If the casualty shows little or no improvement, monitor their vital signs to assess other possible causes, and to ensure that they do not become unconscious.

Unconscious casualty

- If the casualty becomes unconscious and is not breathing sufficiently normally, follow the DRAB/C procedure (see pages 46–7).
- If they are unconscious but breathing as normally as possible in the circumstances, place in the recovery position (see page 48) and call an ambulance.

Note: If you are away from home and have young people with diabetes in your care, ensure that they have sufficient insulin medication with them for the time they are away, and that it is readily accessible should hypoglycemia occur. For more on traveling with young people, see Chapter 2, page 34.

Foreign objects in the eye

On dusty playing surfaces, it is easy for a piece of grit or dust particles to fly up and get caught in the eye. It is also possible for other objects, such as contact lenses (more likely in the older members of your club) or an eyelash to cause discomfort.

Symptoms of a foreign object could be:

- eye redness and eye-watering
- pain and discomfort
- blurred vision
- involuntary blinking, spasming eyelids.

You need to establish that an object is present and try to flush it out before it damages the eye:

- Seat the casualty somewhere in the light where you can see the eye clearly.
- Separate the eyelids gently with the thumb or finger.
- Ask the casualty to look up, down, left and right to see if you can see the object causing the problem.

If you can see the foreign object on the white of the eye:

- Tilt the head back and to the same side as the affected eye, and place a towel on the shoulder.
- Wash the eye with clean water from a glass or, if available, sterile eyewash from an eye bath, pouring the water/eyewash from the bridge of the nose down through the eye toward the shoulder.
- If this fails to flush the object, attempt to use a moist swab or the dampened corner of a tissue to pick up the loose object.

If none of the above works, or the object cannot be located, seek medical attention. If the object is on the iris (i.e., colored part of the eye), do not attempt to remove it, as this may damage the eye. Instead, cover the eye with a patch and arrange for medical treatment at a clinic or emergency department.

A Final Word on the Subject

If you are in any doubt about anything to do with the medical condition of someone, never feel afraid or embarrassed to call 911 and ask for emergency service help. It is better to have expert help quickly on the scene than you trying to be a hero or to have called a false alarm than failed to save a life for the sake of a phone call.

Just remember DRAB/C.

part 2
COACHING AND PLAYER DEVELOPMENT

chapter 4

COACHING

The Role and Impact of the Coach

Ask any top soccer player to name the most important influence on their career and they are likely to refer to a coach, either past or present. Many players would not be where they are today without the help, influence and guidance of one or more coaches. Whether playing soccer at the highest professional level or simply for fun, the importance of a good coach cannot be underestimated. National soccer leagues, through their extensive training program for coaches, have always made it a priority to improve the technical quality of coaching. This reaps rewards on local fields all over the world.

We must remember that coaches, just like teachers, help shape the thoughts, actions, behavior, respect levels and discipline of those they teach, particularly youngsters. Coaches have to be aware that the way they react, what they say and how they approach issues and reach decisions can be mimicked by those in their care.

So the message here is to follow a code of conduct (see Chapter 1). Encourage your team to adopt the codes of conduct for players. Ask parents to help you manage the coaching of their child in a positive and dynamic way. Remember, you cannot please everyone all the time, and there will be occasions when a child or youth becomes impossible to control or teach through no fault of yours. A disruptive element needs to be dealt with in a positive yet firm manner. The backing of a strong committee should ensure that coaches follow good codes of practice, and that parents and players do likewise.

Formulas for Good Coaching

Coaches' checklist

Before any practice or game, coaches should ensure all the following procedures are in place:

- structured warm-up and cool-down
- stretcher and first-aid kit available
- first-aid provider on site
- written first-aid procedures available
- telephone available with list of emergency and contact numbers
- players are wearing shin pads
- plenty of drinks available
- players have removed all jewelry
- players are fit for the activity
- players know the name and location of the venue in case they need to call emergency services.

Coaching Points

- Use guided discovery – ask players if they can see or try another way to improve something.
- Demonstrate.
- Make your point quickly and concisely.
- Give plenty of praise.
- Use the formula: Stop, Question, Demo, Rehearse, Play.

Coaching Qualifications

Becoming a Coach

The first step to becoming a coach is to enroll in a coaching course. Getting on the coaching ladder gives you the opportunity to progress through various coaching qualifications and to enhance your skills and knowledge. Experience is essential for a coach as so much can be learned from the coaching field, whether it is working with other coaches and learning from them or coaching different groups of players with mixed abilities. A successful coach should always be open to new ideas and want to improve their individual skills and knowledge of the game.

U.S. Youth Soccer offers coaching courses through each of its 55-member state associations that are approved by the U.S. Soccer Federation. Courses are available for beginning to advanced coaches, from age-appropriate State Youth Coaching Modules to the important national licenses. Visit www.ussoccer.com for more details.

In Canada, coaches can gain accreditation through the Canadian Soccer Association, which offers a Community Coach Certificate program. Recognizing that most children's coaches are parents often new to the game, the program allows for a coach to complete the children's course in one day and be awarded the designation "Community Coach – Children." More senior level courses are also available. Visit www.canadasoccer.com for details.

Developing Good Habits Early

Discipline

A child brought up to respect the property of others, to be polite, kind, thoughtful and considerate will tend to continue this attitude and approach as they grow up. On the whole, if we can teach children good habits early, we will see them use these social skills throughout their lives.

Soccer players have to socialize, work as a team, give up certain personal agendas and share in group successes and disappointments. All these elements are "character building" and help shape the emotional and mental behavior of an individual, hopefully in a balanced way.

As coaches and guardians of the children at our clubs, we constantly need to remind players of their responsibility for their actions, habits and behavior. How they manage these will determine how socially acceptable they are and how emotionally and mentally balanced they will be throughout life. Naturally, coaches need to be vigilant and help players to recognize ways to handle situations that will benefit them in the future, but without imposing their way as right or the only way.

Here are some hints that coaches may wish to take when dealing with their students:

- Communication is the first step to success for every coach.
- Be clear in your messages – do not allow opportunity for misinterpretation.
- Be proactive – do not hope a problem you see will just go away.
- Use positive language – challenge players to improve rather than punish them.
- Never assume.
- Make all communication seem important.
- Show respect to all players.
- Allow time for everybody.
- Never promise anything you cannot deliver.
- Balance praise with constructive criticism.
- Focus on the correction, not the mistake.
- Learn to be a good listener.
- Learn to be a good questioner.
- Be aware of cultural differences.
- Use players' names and know something of their families and lifestyle.
- Be prepared – start with the end in mind.
- Criticize only performance, not the person.
- Avoid communication when out of control emotionally.
- Make maximum use of informal meeting opportunities.
- Use fun – humor is a great stress reliever.
- Always end communications by clarifying what you have agreed upon.
- Always use the word "we."

- Use the "guided discovery" coaching method whenever possible, which focuses on asking the player to think and say if there is something they could do to improve things. The player, not the coach, solves a problem.

Influential and respected sports psychologists appear to agree that behavior equals personality times environment. So, as a coach it is important that you get the best from your players by adapting your coaching to the individual learning needs of your players in a positive and encouraging way. Make it fun.

chapter 5

WARMING UP

The warm-up before the start of a soccer game or practice takes only a few minutes. A proper warm-up prepares the body for exercise, warms the muscles and enables the body to cope better with the strains of hits and sudden movements that cause injuries. Warming up can prevent serious injury, and the stretching exercises promote agility. If players pull a hamstring or get a back injury, they can be out of soccer for months, and such injuries are often avoidable.

Before you start the warm-up, make sure players are aware of the following essential guidelines:

- Make movements smooth, not jerky.
- Do not overstretch.
- Slight pain is normal; they should feel the muscle stretch.
- They should not feel any severe or stabbing pains; if they do, they must stop immediately.
- Breathe normally during these exercises.
- Repeat each stretch several times and hold for 5–10 seconds.

The Three-phase Warm-up

The following soccer warm-up gradually increases in intensity and follows a logical pattern. You can substitute different activities to form your own workouts, being mindful of the objectives set for each phase.

This warm-up involves three separate phases of work. In each, the intensity of effort is increased from the previous level, giving a gradual progression toward the fully prepared state.

For each phase of the warm-up there are:

- objectives
- suggested activities
- heart rate ranges to achieve objectives.

This warm-up lasts for 20 minutes. Each phase may be reduced if you have less time. You should also tailor the warm-up to the age of the players involved. Younger players, say 10- to 12-year-olds, may require a shorter, less intense warm-up, perhaps just 10 minutes and with more emphasis on fun. It is also important to remember that children lose heat more easily than adults so may require additional clothing to maintain body temperature. For older players, it is important that they are taught good habits regarding the phases of warm-up and the correct methods of stretching. Coaches should not let senior/adult players simply go through the motions of a warm-up – it is a recipe for an early injury.

Phase 1
Objectives

- Gradually raise pulse rate from resting levels
- Preparatory stretching

Content

- Slow jogging, stop, turn, at a low intensity, skipping, backward and sideways jogging

Duration: 5 minutes

Heart rate target for players: 120–140 beats per minute

- Preparatory stretches: calves, hamstrings, quads, hip flexors, lower back – all stretches to be held for only 5 seconds

Duration: 1 minute, 30 seconds

Phase 2
Objectives

- Further increase heart rate through higher intensity activities involving changes of direction and greater distances to cover
- Begin some longer hold stretching on major muscle groups

Content

- Faster jogging followed by striding out, slight changes of direction, high knees, heel flicks

Duration: 5 minutes

Heart rate target for players: 120–160 beats per minute

- Stretches for: calves, hamstrings, quads, adductors, hip flexors, lower back and gluteals – all stretches to be held for 10 seconds

Duration: 2 minutes, 30 seconds

Phase 3

Objectives

- Increase heart rate to final working level
- Full-hold stretches
- Specific movements used in the game

Content

- Striding out followed by sprinting over varying distances, specific movements, e.g., jump and head, turn and sprint, repeated sprint work of short duration, backing off, jockeying

Duration: 5 minutes

Heart rate target for players: 160–200 beats per minute

- Stretches for: calves, hamstrings, quads, hips, adductors and gluteals – all stretches to be held for 10–15 seconds

Duration: 3 minutes

Following this warm-up, players should return to some high-intensity sprinting and specific movements such as jumping, heading, turning and sprinting, jockeying to ensure full readiness for the game.

Warm-up for Under-10s

Stretching exercises are not necessary for this age group, and the warm-up need only be brief. Some jogging, swinging of the arms, twists of the hips or other movements to loosen up will suffice. It is, however, important to do some warm-up and cool-down routines – albeit short in duration and concentration – to build discipline in youngsters for later life.

Warm-up for 10- to 12-year-olds

A 10-minute warm-up is all that is necessary, and overstretching at this age can even be harmful. Perform the first phase of the adult warm-up (see page 82) consisting of jogging followed by one round of *gentle* stretching with 5-second holds. Follow this with a few minutes practicing ball control skills – passing and movement exercises are particularly good.

Warm-up for 13-year-olds and Over

Start your soccer warm-up with some gentle exercise, such as jogging. The aim is to raise the heart rate to around 120 beats per minute. Then perform some *gentle* stretches, holding for about 5 seconds on each stretch. Work with a ball in a team game of some kind that blends exercise and stretches, gently increasing heart rate. A particular favorite of mine involves teams of four, split into two players (numbered 1 and 3) opposite the other two (numbered 2 and 4), 30 feet (9 m) apart. Player 1 passes the ball to player 2 and follows the pass to join the back of the line. Simply rotate all the players. Different drills can be completed, such as simple passes, chipped passes and running with the ball. You could pop a cone or two down in the middle as an obstacle for players to go around. Another idea for four players is to get one player to stand in each corner of a 30-foot (10 m) square. Player 1 passes the ball to an available player and follows the pass in to take their place. This enjoyable, high-tempo exercise includes all the elements necessary to prepare players for the game ahead.

Pre-game Warm-up Drills

Here are some more fun warm-up activities. They can all be carried out within an area of 30 feet × 60 feet (9 m × 18 m) or 30 feet × 90 feet (9 m × 27 m), depending on the age group. Remember to stop after every two or three minutes for players to stretch muscle groups or have a drink.

Throw and Catch

Get the players to jog within the whole area, throwing and catching a ball (a bit like football passing). Use three or four soccer balls in the grid.

- For very young kids, work within a smaller 30-foot × 60-foot (9 m × 18 m) area. Also, remember that young players may not be able to catch or are perhaps a little frightened of the ball, so let them hand the ball to a teammate and run off to find someone else to take a ball from. Alternatively, they could pass the ball with a foot.

- Progress this activity for older players, so that the throw is for a header or a volley, or a thigh control and volley, etc. Each time, the thrower gives the ball back to the partner so that everyone gets to head, volley and so on.

- To ensure players get maximum benefit from these exercises, encourage them to move into another 30-foot × 30-foot (10 m × 10 m) grid rather than stay in the same area.

Sprinting and Jogging

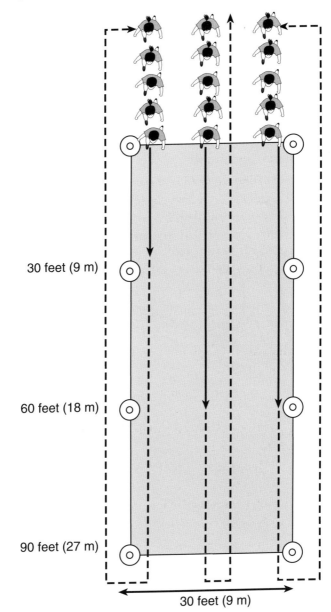

30 feet (9 m)

60 feet (18 m)

90 feet (27 m)

30 feet (9 m)

This is designed for older kids and adults (11 a side). Place cones at 30-foot (10 m) intervals over 90 feet (27 m) in length. Split the team into three groups of five in lines at one end of the grid. You can use a mixture of short sprints, jogs and dynamic stretches over 30 and 60 feet (9 and 18 m). The final 30 and 60 feet (9 and 18 m) should be used for recovery – either walking or light jogging.

Here are some suggestions for four exercises:

- A short sprint – do this twice.
- Sideways crab sprints – do this twice.
- Sweep-the-floor type run – do this twice.
- A high knee sprint – do this twice.

Ensure players do the full recovery jog through to the end and back down to join the line. Note the direction so that players don't bump into each other. Do the four exercise repetitions and then allow players to have a minute of static stretching and a drink. One final note: let a player cover 30 feet (9 metres) before the next player goes.

Here are a few ideas for other exercises that the players can do.

- Sprint 30 feet (9 m) – jog
- Turn left knee "out" 30 feet (9 m) – jog
- Turn right knee "out" 30 feet (9 m) – jog
- As above, only turn knee "in" 30 feet (9 m) – jog
- High knees 60 feet (18 m) – jog
- Swivel hips right and left (swing arms in sync with hip rotations) 60 feet (18 m) – jog
- Side steps right – three strides – then left then back to right and so on – forwards 60 feet (18 m) – jog
- Side steps right – three strides – then left then back to right and so on – backwards 60 feet (18 m) – jog
- Heels (bring heels up to bottom) 60 feet (18 m) – jog
- Sprint 60 feet (18 m) – jog

To turn the knee "in" or "out," players bring their knee up vertically as they jog forward and turn it in (across them) or out.

Passing in Zones
Younger children

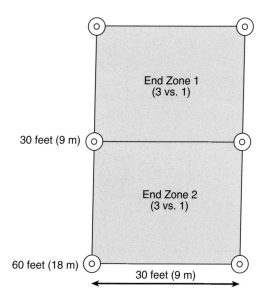

For children under 10 in mini soccer, use the 30-feet × 60-feet (9 m × 18 m) grid split into two equal zones. You can work with the ball in an enjoyable way that will also tune players into the game.

Split the team: in each zone put three against one (one in a vest) or four against one, depending on numbers. The idea is for the three or four players in zone 1 to pass the ball around within the zone while the vested player tries to intercept the ball. After two or three passes, a player in zone 1 passes the ball into zone 2 where the game continues in the same way. After one minute, change the vested player.

NOTE: for the very young, the coach should be the vested player and cannot tackle or intercept.

The coach should help the players by making it obvious, with their position and angle, which is the best pass for the player with the ball to make. The coach can easily cover both zones and should not insist that young players pass any set number of times before sending the ball into the other zone.

Older children

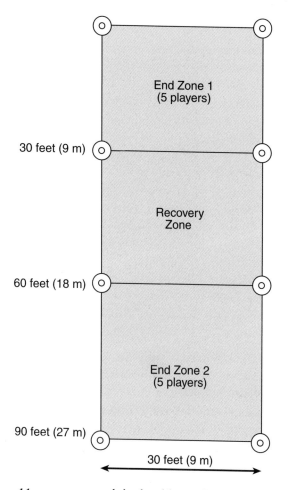

Children over 11 years up to adult should use the 30-foot × 90-foot (9 m × 27 m) grid divided into three zones. Split the team: put five in zone 1 and the same in zone 2. Four extra players in vests pair-up – one pair will operate in zone 1 and the other in zone 2. When one pair is not working to intercept the ball in a zone they should "recover" in the recovery zone.

The idea is for the players in zone 1 to pass the ball around within the zone while the vested players try to intercept it. After three or four passes, a player in zone 1 passes or chips the ball into zone 2 where the game continues in the same way. The players in the recovery zone cannot intercept at this stage. If the vested players succeed in intercepting the ball, get them to switch with other players. If they do not succeed, change the vested players after two minutes.

The coach can progress this exercise by asking the vested players in the recovery zone to try and intercept the pass from one zone to another. This encourages non-vested players on both sides to see an opportunity to pass, and the receiving players to move to accept a good, safe pass. Further progression can include lifting the restriction on the number of passes in a zone before transfer of the ball. This encourages the players to see and react to forward passing opportunities.

Whatever the age group of the players, this drill acts as a great game warm-up or practice drill. Every player is involved and can learn many things: how to receive a ball, when to pass, where to pass, who to shut down, communication, awareness of others and much more besides. Remember to change the vested players often and offer drinks as appropriate.

Mini-game

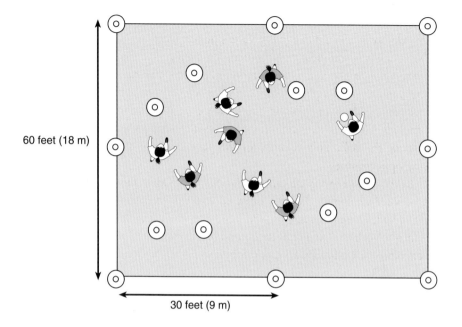

60 feet (18 m)

30 feet (9 m)

This is another closing warm-up drill that kids and adults love. Use a 60-foot × 60-foot (18m × 18m) grid. Split the team in half with one side wearing a distinctive colored vest. The aim is to win a point or goal simply by passing the ball through one of the gates – marked by two space markers or poles – to a teammate. The coach – on the outside – needs to have a ball with them always to keep play moving. This encourages passing, tackling, defending, switching play and many other key elements of the game while generating a lot of fun and friendly competition.

Conclusion

In a small area, a coach can conduct a warm-up session that involves all the elements of running, stretching, teamwork, concentration/focus and ball play in a highly effective way. All the exercises should include regular breaks for static stretching or having a drink.

For children under 10, the whole warm-up period should be around 15 minutes. Children aged 11–14 can warm up for up to 30 minutes, while anything up to 40 minutes can be allowed for adults.

chapter 6
COACHING THE BASIC SKILLS

This chapter is designed to help coaches get the right techniques across to players. Teaching good techniques in the basic soccer skills, especially to the very young, is of paramount importance if they are to be good players in the future. Good coaches are not there to try and coach flair and panache but to help players improve their technique and become confident in using their natural abilities.

Players should have fun while learning these skills. Don't scold a player for not getting the technique right. Instead, praise them for their efforts. Taking time to teach basic skills will bring many rewards for coaches as they slowly start to see the young players in their care blossom.

Kicking the Ball

Soccer kicking techniques range from basic shooting and passing skills to advanced techniques, such as bending the ball around a wall and penalty kicks. It is important to start with the basics – ensure that players master the key skills using the instep and inside of the foot. Over 50 percent of youth players use incorrect techniques, which results in inaccurate passes that do not have the right pace or stay on the ground.

The Instep

The instep, the part of the foot where the laces are, provides both power and control – it is used for the majority of kicking in a game. The most common mistake made by beginners is to use the toe. Not only is this painful if somebody tackles hard when they are trying to kick, but it can also be very inaccurate. The advantage of the instep is that it presents a flat surface to the ball, and can also be used to make the ball swerve, curve and dip.

The nonkicking leg provides support, and should be bent as players kick. When we want to keep the ball on the ground, the head is down, over the ball. The follow-through should be long and smooth, and another useful tip is to approach the kick slightly from the side.

The Lofted Kick

The lofted kick is used to play the long ball, cross the ball into the penalty area, and to clear the ball from defense. It is the only technique for lifting the ball into the air with real power.

A goalkeeper with good kicking technique can create an attacking situation with good length and accuracy of a kick. Goalkeepers should regularly practice this type of kick as goal kicks are a regular occurrence in games.

Coaching Tips

- To achieve height, players should lean back as they strike the ball.
- To bend the ball, players should kick the ball below the midline and slightly to one side.
- To keep balance, players should place the nonkicking foot slightly in front of the ball instead of level with it, and put their arms out.
- It is important to obtain distance from the kick as well as height – the object is to kick the ball high enough to clear any opposing players, but extra height is not necessary and will reduce the length of the kick.

Corners

The lofted kick is generally used for taking corners, preferably with some spin applied to swerve the ball (*see* below). Corners are excellent goal scoring opportunities because the ball can be crossed directly into the most dangerous area of the field, in front of the goal. A well-directed header from a corner kick is generally all that is needed to score a goal. Corners should be practiced and involve players moving into target areas – namely near-post, penalty spot and far-post (*see* "Crosses" on page 96).

It is worth working on strategy for corner kicks in your team's coaching sessions. All too often I watch teams who only ever kick the ball into a crowded goalmouth. Apart from being predictable, it can only have a 50 percent chance of success, and with a goalkeeper able to jump and catch the ball the odds are probably less.

Coaching Tips

- Do you want corners to swing in toward the goal or out away from the goal? This will require a corner on the right to be taken by a player using their left foot or right foot, respectively.

- Work on passing the ball firmly into a player at the near-post who can direct the ball away from the goal for a shot by an incoming teammate.

- Play the short corner to a fullback who has timed their run late to catch the opposition by surprise.

- By varying your corners, you can create many more goal scoring opportunities.

Crosses

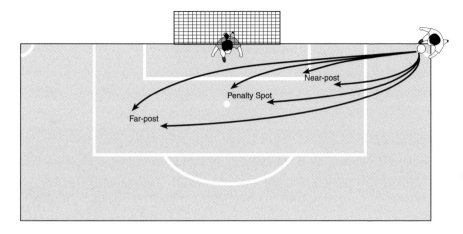

There are three main types of crosses:

1. The near-post cross
2. The cross to the penalty spot
3. The far-post cross

At the **near-post** the attacker tries to get in front of the defender, ideally with a run toward the goal to obtain momentum. Depending on the type of pass made, the player at the near-post can get a "flick on" to divert the ball crossed in or control the ball with a returned pass. Often the kicking technique here is a short "chip" into the near-post or perhaps a low-driven strike/pass into the feet of the near-post runner.

The **cross to the penalty spot** should be met by a player powerfully and confidently running into the box from the edge of the 18-yard area. A coaching tip here is to practice timing of the run and to be aware of the curve on the ball. For instance, a right-footed cross from the right wing will often curve away from the goal. Therefore it is more successful if the run is late to meet the ball rather than early, risking getting under the ball or the ball curving behind you.

At the **far-post** the attacker usually tries to get behind the defense, on the blind side. This type of cross tends to favor taller players who can jump high over the defense, whereas shorter players are better placed at the near-post.

Both corner kicks and general crossing of the ball should be regularly brought into coaching sessions for all age groups. Strategically, these can be potent weapons in the team's armory, so practicing different moves is well worth it. My advice for coaching corners and crosses is to mix it up. Try short and long crosses. Try angled back passes and chain passes across the field. Coach good tactical movement in the goal area, and so on. Have a few set routines and get your corner-taker to signify which technique or type of cross they intend to make.

Chipping

The chip is a kicking technique used to lift the ball quickly over short distances. The disadvantage of the chip over the lofted kicking technique is that it lacks power. The advantages are that lift can be produced quickly, and that the backspin generated from this method causes the ball to slow down on hitting the ground.

The chip uses a stabbing or chopping motion in which the lower part of the foot, but not the toe, makes contact low down on the ball. The knee of the kicking foot is bent, and high at the end of the follow-through. As for the lofted kick, it is best to lean back slightly, but with the head looking down at the ball. A useful tip is to place the nonkicking foot slightly behind the ball.

Learning how to take a cross in soccer requires mastering several different skills:

- The kicking technique needs to be correct.
- The player must have vision and awareness of whom to aim the cross for.
- The player must be able to create space for the cross under pressure from defenders.

The kicking technique for crossing the ball is to use the instep, getting underneath the ball, and preferably to put some spin on the ball to bend it away from the goalkeeper or to put curl on the ball to keep it in play. This makes the cross harder to intercept. Sometimes, a player will find themselves having to cross the ball from a very square position close to the touchline. In this case it might be necessary to use the area around the big toe for kicking the ball in order to keep it in play.

Corner and crossing drills

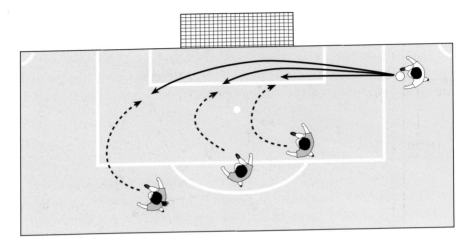

For the very young – up to 8 or 9 years of age – use a light or soft ball to throw into an area for a header or shot at goal. Start by having no goalkeeper so that the youngsters enjoy the experience of scoring. Put the players in groups of three and work on their movement to meet the ball being thrown in and the correct techniques for heading (downward) and striking the ball (keeping it low enough to hit the target). Also work on the timing of their runs to meet the ball, rather than getting too far forward so the ball goes over their heads. Mix up the throws to the near- and far-posts as well as the penalty spot area. Gradually introduce a goalkeeper as the players become more confident and able.

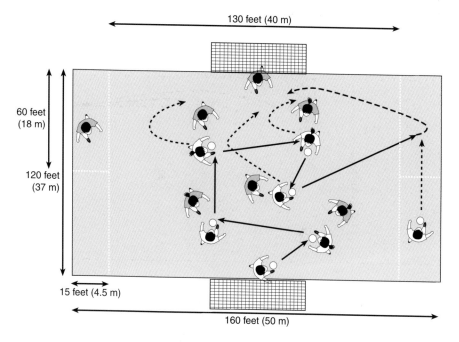

Another drill is to position cones down the line of the 18-yard area on both sides of the field and about another 15–30 feet (4.5–9 m) or so in. This will create a channel for a wide player to run into before crossing. Line your defenders and attackers up about 90 feet (27 m) out from the defending goal. Start the drill with midfield players in the center circle passing the ball around. After three or four passes, play the ball into one of the channels for a winger or fullback to run on to. Their job is to run the ball through the channel and whip a cross in. The attackers must support the play and get on the end of the cross while midfield players support them for any short clearances. Defenders will have to retreat and defend the cross while the goalkeeper is forced to decide whether to come and collect the cross or stay and defend the goal. Practice this from both right and left wings.

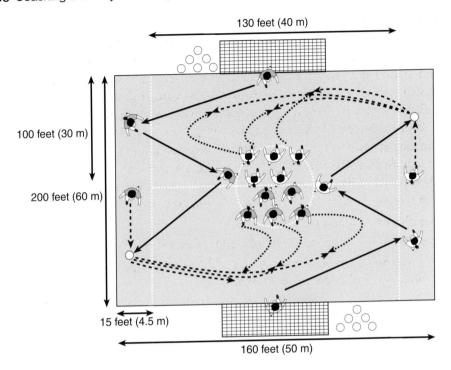

A drill for older players – 12-year-olds and above – is the highly intensive and fast-paced crossing-rotation drill. This must be high tempo but with regular breaks for recovery and drinks. Work in a 130-foot × 200-foot (40 m × 60 m) area with a channel down each side. Split the outfield players into two sides with distinctive colored vests and position in the center of the field, with two players on each side in the channel, as shown. Goalkeepers start the drill with a throw to one of their teammates in the channel (in the fullback position). The ball is passed into the feet of one of the attacking group who comes short for the pass and then lays it out into the channel for the winger to run on to and cross. Three attacking players make runs to meet the cross with a header or shot. The other side now become the attackers and the process begins again on the other side of the field.

Once you have worked on crosses from the right (clockwise), progress the drill to work from the left (counterclockwise). A further progression is for the player receiving the ball from the goalkeeper to act as a defender on the opposite cross or for two players of the opposition to act as defenders, tracking the runs of the attackers. This offers overload for the attackers and improves decision-making of the runs and crosses.

Free Kicks

Taking free kicks is an important skill that requires awareness of soccer tactics as well as sound technique. Free kicks provide an opportunity to control play, and around the penalty area they are goal scoring opportunities. The coach should plan several attacking set plays with the team, including free kicks from different angles, so that each player knows what they should be doing.

When taking free kicks around the penalty area, the fewer touches before shooting at the goal the better. Teams and coaches should aim for a direct shot or a single pass before shooting, because set plays involving more than one pass allow plenty of time for the defense to organize and close down.

In training, work on a variety of set plays such as:

- a direct shot around or over the wall
- a pass to the side of the wall followed by a shot at the goal
- a chip over the wall toward the edge of the 6-yard box, aiming for a player to head into goal or control and shoot.

In the midfield, free kicks are opportunities to build an attack. Look to take the free kick quickly if there is a player with space, but otherwise allow time for your own team to push forward.

In defense, free kicks are similar to goal kicks with the choice of playing a short or a long ball. This will depend on your team's strengths and tactics, but the ball should always be cleared from dangerous positions. This usually means long, high and wide kicks.

Bending the ball

Bending or swerving the ball is one of the most exciting soccer kicking techniques. Brazilians, such as Pelé, were famous for making the ball bend around a defensive wall, and this is one of David Beckham's hallmarks. This skill is important in many areas of soccer, such as shots at goal around defenders who are obscuring the goalkeeper's view, corner kicks, crosses into the box and passing the ball around opponents.

There are two main methods: using the outside of the foot to swerve the ball away from you, or using the inside of the foot to bend the ball inward. Swerve is produced by kicking the ball off-center on the opposite side to the side you want the ball to swerve to. For example, if a player wants to bend the ball from right to left with their right foot, they should make contact with the ball on the right side using the inside of the foot. To make the ball bend away from them from left to right, they should kick the ball on the left side using the outside of the foot.

Volleying

Volley technique is a difficult soccer skill to master, but volleys have produced many spectacular goals. Volleying requires the player to strike through the ball, keeping the knee level or over the ball rather than under it, which has the effect of keeping the ball on a straight trajectory.

As well as goal scoring, volleys can be used for passing, and kicking the ball away from danger. In tight situations, it is often better for a defender to volley the ball away than try to control it at a difficult height.

Keeping the ball down is one of the important aspects of volleying technique. As with all kicking skills, watching the ball and keeping the head down helps, but it is important to try to keep the knee over the ball.

Coaching Tips

One of the secrets of great volleys is the swivel motion.

- The player starts from a square position with both feet a comfortable distance apart.
- Then, without moving their feet, the player twists the upper body to the right until the left shoulder is facing directly in front.
- Next, the player twists back until the right shoulder is facing in front.
- This can be practiced without a ball.
- For a left-footed volley, twist first to the left and then to the right.

Passing the Ball

Passing techniques are vital for keeping possession and controlling the game, and many parts of the foot can be used. Technically, any ball that reaches a player on the same team is a pass – be it a kick, header or even a throw-in – so nearly all the sections in this chapter relate to passing (and controlling and receiving the ball, see below, which are equally important). However, there are a couple of specific points that should be made.

Inside of the Foot "Push" Pass

The simplest and best technique for short passes is with the head over the ball, the body well balanced, and the ball kicked with the inside of the foot, which is the flattest part of the foot. This is known as the "push" pass. Sometimes this technique is used for short-range shots at goal, and even for taking penalties, because of its reliability. The disadvantage is the lack of power. Accurate short passes with supporting runs into space allow a team to keep possession and build an attack.

Coaching Tips: The "Push" Pass

- Get the player to face the target so the ball and target are in a straight line.
- Place the "plant" foot alongside the ball, with toes pointing toward the target.
- The head should be over the ball, looking down, and both knees slightly bent.
- Teach the proper motion by first having the player place their striking foot flat against the back of the ball, pushing the ball toward the target and following through.
- Now ask them to do the same, but this time taking one step into the ball. This step provides power to the pass. If the pass goes into the air it means it was struck below the midline of the ball.

Passing Drills

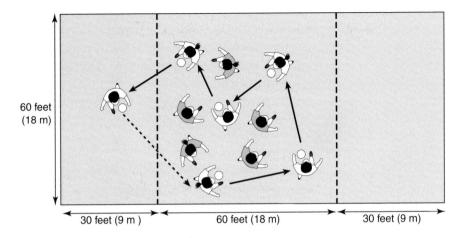

60 feet
(18 m)

30 feet (9 m)　60 feet (18 m)　30 feet (9 m)

There are many soccer drills for passing skills, and one of the most enjoyable is a five-a-side game played within a 60-foot × 120-foot (18 m × 37 m) area. Zone off two end zones, 30 feet × 60 feet (9 m × 18 m) as shown. Quite simply, play five against five in the middle zone, and a goal is scored when a pass is made from a player in the middle to a teammate running into an end zone. Soccer is a 360-degree game, so players should be allowed to score with a pass into either end zone. Restart each time with a feed from the side into the middle zone. This drill encourages players to create and move into space to receive a pass, and others to move to open up opportunities to score a goal or point.

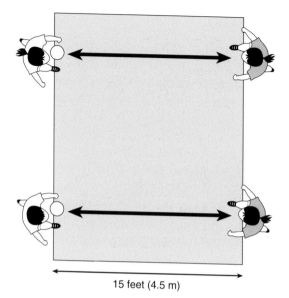

15 feet (4.5 m)

Here's a passing drill for young players. Pair up players opposite each other. One passes to the other, who controls the ball and passes it back to their partner. Get the players to move out to 60 feet (18 m) apart. As the passes are being made and on the call of the coach, get one side to gradually come in, 15 feet (4.5 m) at a time, until the players are passing just 15 feet (4.5 m).

This drill has several skill components within it: the cushion control, pace, and accuracy of the passing and receiving. Getting the players to move in closer and then further away helps them grasp the art of weighting the ball with greater or lesser power. Remember to add communication in the drill and get the players to praise their partner if they do something well.

A progression for the drill is to get players on either side to swap with the player to their right or left each time they pass the ball. This adds receiving the ball on the move, is a great warm-up exercise and brings some lively fun and enjoyment to the drill, especially when the players are only 15 feet (4.5 m) apart.

Heading the Ball

Heading techniques are vital in the game of soccer. The team that dominates in the air can win the ball in the danger zone in front of the 6-yard box when both defending and attacking, and can win the ball from long goal kicks. Heading skills also enable a team to use the long ball tactic effectively for flick-ons and nod-downs. This can very quickly turn a defensive situation into a goal scoring one.

Coaching Tips

The correct part of the head to use is the forehead. This is the hardest and flattest part of the head, and with the eyes open on contact will give better control and greater power.

You often see youngsters playing soccer who can play the ball well on the ground, but are not confident when the ball is played in the air. Often the problem is a fear of getting hurt, but once they learn to head the ball properly using the forehead, there is no danger.

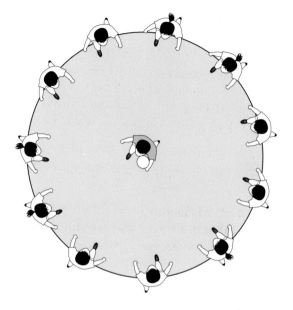

A useful way to introduce players under 8 years old to heading is to play some fun games. One I particularly like is the head-catch game with a soft, spongy ball or an indoor soft soccer (looks like a big tennis ball). Arrange your players in a circle not too far away from you and close enough for a gentle throw of the ball to reach them.

The coach stands in the middle with the ball and moves around the circle. As the ball travels to a player, the coach calls out if it is to be caught or headed. The coach can mix things up by going in different directions and choosing players at random. To progress this game, the coach can ask the players to do the opposite things to the call – so a catch becomes a header and vice versa.

Defensive Heading

Defensive heading techniques enable a player to direct the ball upward in such situations as clearing the ball from defense. Any qualified coach will tell you that the key ingredients to a good defensive header are "high, long and wide."

Coaching Tips

- The key to the defensive header is to start with the forehead underneath the ball, so that the head can move upward to attack the ball.
- The player's eyes must remain below the ball, so that at the moment the forehead makes contact with the ball, the head is moving upward.
- The player should use their legs to push upward just before heading the ball as this helps to obtain good distance.

A useful and fun game for beginners and more experienced players is heading the soccer ball over a volleyball net. Since the ball has to be directed upward to clear the net, it is particularly good practise for defensive heading. It is also a great way for players to learn control and direction.

Attacking Heading

Attacking heading techniques are used for directing the ball downward to score goals and win the ball in the air. The key to the attacking header is to get the eyes focused on the ball and to get the forehead over the ball, thus attacking the ball from above.

Beginners often have trouble timing the header, and end up hitting the nose or the top of the head, so coaches should start young children with a soft ball. It is important to teach players to watch the ball carefully. Balance is another point to watch – try to encourage beginners to get their feet into position early so that they are behind the ball. A useful drill to help young players learn the technique of a downward attacking header is to use a target on the ground – something like a cone or circle of space-markers a few feet away. Pair up players opposite each other and have a competition to see who can be the first to hit the target five times.

More able and older players should work on meeting crosses on the move, so that their momentum helps add power to the header, and to avoid being caught static by defenders. Players should aim to head the ball downward into areas where goalkeepers find it most difficult to get down.

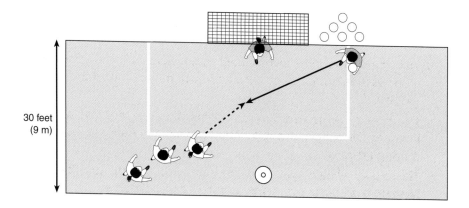

A good drill for this is to start with a line of players on the edge of the 18-yard area where it meets the "D." The coach stands on the corner of the 6-yard area where it meets the base line to the penalty spot area and throws a ball toward the penalty spot for a player to run in and meet the ball with an attacking header. Put a goalkeeper in goal to help the attacking players head the ball wide of the goalkeeper but inside the posts. The coach can move up the 6-yard line to vary the angles of delivery. As players become more experienced, crosses can be delivered from wide areas for attackers to meet the ball. The next progression is to introduce a defender or two.

Several factors help players obtain power when attacking a header. The shoulders can be pushed forward and the back arched before attacking the ball. The upper body should be kept in a straight line, not falling away to the side, and much of the power comes from the neck muscles. It is very important to be positive and always to focus on the ball.

Diving Headers

The diving header technique gives a player that extra edge and versatility to reach the ball first and to get a head on crosses that would otherwise be missed. This is particularly true at the near-post where the attacker is trying to get in front of the defender.

The diving header requires getting both feet off the ground, and a jump toward the ball. The player should be almost horizontal as they head the ball, using their forehead (as always). Generally, takeoff is from only one foot because the diving header is usually attempted on the run. Players must keep their eyes open as this will help to direct the header goalward.

Most players find the dive the most difficult part of this technique. Players who are having problems should practice without the ball. Put a low hurdle down, such as a large bag, a couple of twigs, or even a player crouched down if you can find a volunteer! Get the player to jump the hurdle without hesitating. Then try the same thing with someone serving the ball so that the player jumps over the hurdle to head the ball.

Dribbling Skills

Dribbling is all about close control and confidence. Improving close control and dribbling skills in soccer is vital for a player to be able to create space, keep possession and beat defenders. Close control is essential for every player on the field, including the goalkeeper. It generally refers to running with the ball and dribbling skills, but it can also include the first touch, and control with the foot, thigh, chest and head. Close control is a vital part of soccer coaching.

Running with the Ball

Running with the ball is the first stage of close control. The aim is to keep the ball within your control without needing to break your stride. This technique uses the instep or, more commonly, the outside of the foot, which gives greater fluency of movement and ball control. On the field of play, running with the ball often occurs when a wide player has got past a defender and has 60 to 90 feet (18 to 27 m) of clear space in front of them. They need to cover the ground quickly and still be in a position to deliver a cross for the attacking teammates. Improving close control also requires turning ability (see below).

Coaches should encourage players to begin dribbling at slow speeds, and then gradually build up speed. A simple exercise to help learn running with the ball is to build an obstacle course with cones or other markers placed at varying distances apart, and at different angles to each other. The object is to run with the ball as quickly as possible from cone to cone, but coming to a complete stop at each cone. This teaches close control, running, accelerating and stopping with the ball.

Another popular drill is to place two lanes of space-markers in a straight line 30 feet (9 m) apart and up to 120 feet (37 m) long. At each end of the lane place four space-markers in a 30-foot × 30-foot (9 m × 9 m) square where the players wait. Split your players into two groups: one group at one end in a square; the other in the other square. The first player runs the ball through the lane and at the end passes diagonally to a player waiting in the square who repeats the exercise. The key factors are a good first touch on receiving the ball out and in front of you into your path, to knock the ball no more than 30 feet (9 m) at a time in a straight line and be able to make a good quality pass at the end of the run. Try to get players to use the instep or outside of the foot for greater control. Keep this going until all players have grasped the drill.

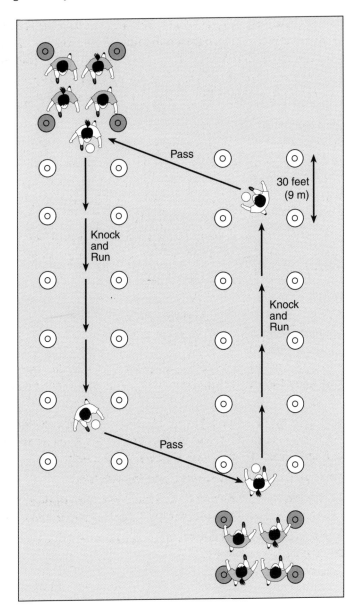

If you have enough players, set up another similar area and spilt the players into two teams. Each team player must have a minimum of four touches of the ball on the way out turn, and a minimum of four touches on the way back before passing to the next player. The winners are the team who go through the exercise, get back to their starting positions first and sit down or raise their hands.

The Body Swerve

The body swerve is a close control, dribbling skill used for running at and beating defenders, and creating space to shoot or pass the ball. The aim of the body swerve is to fool the defender into moving the wrong way. In the game of soccer the body swerve is one of the most effective dribbling tricks, and was superbly demonstrated by the late Sir Stanley Matthews.

The body swerve builds upon basic turning skills (see below), and coaches should make sure that young players are able to turn with the ball under close control to the left and right.

Coaching Tips

- With the ball on the right foot, the player should dip their left shoulder, and start to transfer body weight as if they are going to the left.

- However, instead of turning to the left, the player should quickly lean to the right, transferring weight to this side and using the left foot as a springboard to accelerate away to the right.

- The movement is reversed when using the left foot.

- Players should be encouraged to use both feet during drills, otherwise they will become predictable to defenders in the game.

- Speed is important – both acceleration and the ability to change speeds quickly.

Training drills for the body swerve include one-against-one exercises in front of the goal. The object need not always be to go past the defender, but could be just to make space to shoot. The slalom is a good exercise for training when you are on your own, remembering to dip the shoulder.

Selling the Fake

There are many different types of fakes a player can use to confuse a defender. The objective is always to send an opponent the wrong way, take them by surprise or force them to make a tackle.

Defenders do not know what an attacker is going to do – they have to keep watch on the ball, be aware of their position and try to force attackers into safe areas away from the goal. Attacking players should be coached to remember that they have this upper hand and initiative over their opponents.

Leaving the ball

The simplest fake is leaving the ball. This is an opportunistic move in which the ball is typically allowed to pass through the legs to another player who is in a better position.

The step-over

This trick often sends a defender one way, making it difficult for them to recover. It requires the attacker to transfer their body weight to one side, moving the foot toward the ball as if turning to that side, but at the last moment stepping over the ball, and continuing in the same or opposite direction. A variation is to move the foot around the ball instead of over it, taking it in the opposite direction. Again, defenders will be sent one way, making it hard to shift direction and put a tackle in.

Stop-start

Another effective fake is the stop-start move. The technique is to step on the ball with the sole of one foot, and then kick the ball forward with the other foot. The aim is to do this as one movement without actually stopping. Defenders will often be forced to make a tackle and be caught off-balance.

Faking drills

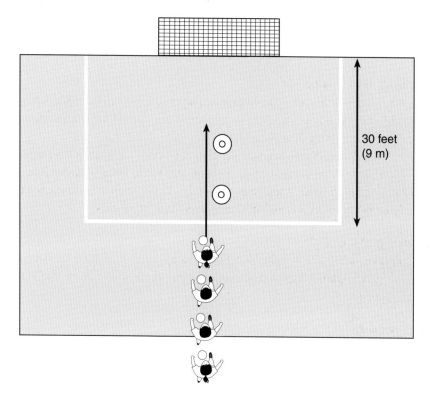

30 feet
(9 m)

Each week set 10 minutes aside to get your players to practice a trick or fake. For 5- to 7-year-olds, place up to three space-markers in front of an empty goal 30 feet (9 m) out. The space-markers can be placed in a variety of formations such as a zigzag, straight line or slalom. Each player runs the ball toward the space-markers and tries a trick to pass them and fire home a goal. This has a terrific outcome for the young players: they learn different types of fakes, they gain confidence and they score goals. Ask players to practice during the week and to show you the results at the next practice.

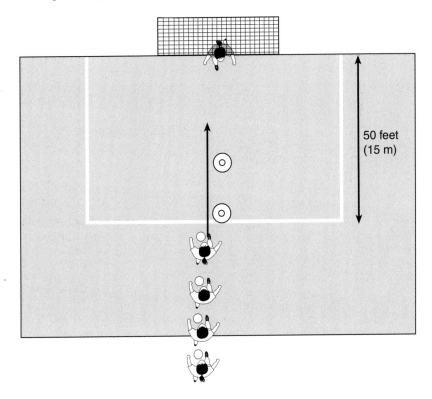

For 8- to 10-year-olds you can introduce a goalkeeper in a mini-goal. Players still have to beat the space-markers with fakes and tricks but now have to decide whether to shoot or take on the goalkeeper.

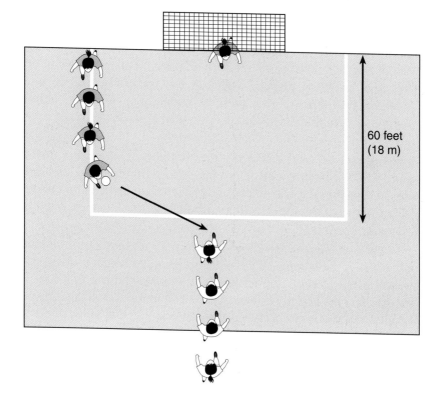

For 11-year-olds and above, introduce a defender and consider attackers working from a static start in a straight line or perhaps a rolling passed ball from an angle. Mix it up to bring realism into the session.

Ball Juggling

Soccer juggling skills and tricks are not just a means of showing off. They are excellent training methods for improving ball control, balance, first touch and general technique. Many coaches recommend starting a coaching session, whether for youth or adult players, with five minutes of ball juggling.

Juggling can be done using the top of the foot, the sides of the foot, the thigh or the head. There are also a number of tricks that involve throwing the ball up and catching it. The ball can be caught using the top of the foot, the thigh, the chest and even the back of the neck.

The goal with juggling is simple – players try to beat their personal best score of how many touches they can make without letting the ball fall to the ground. Beginners can start by juggling with the foot, and allowing the ball to bounce once between touches. They should progress quickly to not allowing the ball to bounce at all.

Controlling the Ball

A skillful first touch gives a player time and space in which to move with the ball or find the best pass. Players who let the ball run away from them are always under pressure to recover control of the ball. This allows time for opponents to close them down, and often means they lose control of the ball completely.

There are a number of ways of controlling the ball, depending on the situation the player is in and the part of the body they use.

Foot Control

Control with the foot when receiving the ball requires a soft touch. The technique is simply to withdraw the foot on contact with the ball, often referred to as "cushioning" the ball. The amount of cushion depends on how quickly the ball is coming. Players should move to the ball, not wait for it to come to them, and keep their eyes firmly on the ball.

The inside of the foot is the safest and most common technique for receiving the ball. It allows the ball to be taken on the move, whereas the old-fashioned method of trapping the ball with the sole (underneath) of the foot involves stopping the ball dead. In a match context, stopping the ball can give the opposition time to get into good defensive positions and/or time to put pressure on the player with the ball and to tackle. Receiving the ball with the top of the foot and outside of the foot are more difficult skills, but the principles of relaxing and withdrawing the foot on impact are the same.

Coaching Tips

Receiving the ball (under-7s)

- On receipt of the ball, relax the receiving foot so the ball stops about one step away (so you can quickly take one step and strike it).

- Be sure the receiving foot is slightly off the ground – if too low the ball will "bobble" up. Use the arch of the foot to cushion the ball.

- If you want the ball to go to the left or right (instead of straight in front) you must angle your foot in the direction you want it to go.

Receiving the ball (8 years and over)

- While waiting to receive a pass, keep your knees slightly bent and stay on the balls of your feet so you are ready to move quickly to either side. If you raise your heels off the ground about half an inch, you are on the balls of your feet.

- When the ball is kicked, quickly notice its direction – is it going to your left or right or straight at you? It is useful to bounce gently from one foot to the other to help you adjust to the direction of the ball and be ready to move in any direction.

- Move toward the ball.

- Stop the ball in front of you or to the left or right, depending on where your opponent is. If an opponent is not close by, cushion the ball so it moves about one step away from you and in the direction you want to go so you can quickly step up to the ball and pass or shoot it.

- If an opponent is close by, try to cushion or take the ball in a direction that rolls it away from your opponent and into an open area, giving you time and space to dribble, pass or shoot.

- Good players can receive and make passes with both feet and without having to think too long and hard about it.

Chest Control

Chest control skill in soccer is often required to bring the ball under control from awkward heights. It can be used to pass the ball and drop the ball to the feet, and to deflect the ball through all angles, even behind.

In all chest control skills, the best technique is to present the whole of the chest to the ball, rather than attempting to take the ball sideways on. Naturally, the greater the surface meeting the ball, the more control the player will have. The ball can be deflected to the side by turning the upper body on contact. When passing the ball with the chest, the chest and back are kept rigid. The breastplate, or sternum, is the hard part of the chest and the area used to generate power for a chest pass. Players will use the power and speed of the ball coming to them to rebound it into the path of a teammate. To stop or "kill" the ball, the chest and back should be relaxed to cushion the ball and angle it down to the feet. This technique can also be used when the ball is bouncing upward from the ground.

Thigh Control

Thigh control is required when the ball arrives at awkward heights above the knee, but too low to head or chest down. The key is to withdraw the thigh on impact, similar to the cushion technique mentioned above. It is also possible to deflect the ball by rotating the thigh and glancing the ball to the side. Only a small nudge is usually necessary to guide the ball, and coaches should encourage players to deflect the ball and turn in one movement. By making the thigh more rigid, a player can hit the ball up in a controlled way for, say, a volley or drilled pass.

Head Control

The aim of the controlled header is to drop the ball to the feet as soon as possible. Players should make contact with the ball in the centre of the forehead, and use their whole body as a shock absorber to cushion the ball. In particular, knees should be bent to drop the upper body, and the back should arch on impact. The head must be upward when the player receives the ball, in order to cushion it. If they try to head the ball down, they will knock it to the ground, but will not be able to take the pace off the ball. Players must let gravity drop the ball to their feet.

Control Drills

All the types of control listed above develop with practice and should be introduced regularly to training sessions from a very early age. Here are just a few drills I use for the various age groups.

Soccer tennis

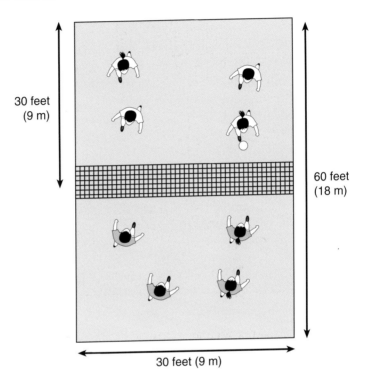

30 feet
(9 m)

60 feet
(18 m)

30 feet (9 m)

This superb training ground drill incorporates every ball control technique mentioned in this chapter. It is a game designed for players who have developed reasonable skill and control of the ball. You do not need a tennis court – any suitable area will do. For the net, a coach could purchase a garden tennis or badminton net, use two poles with rope and some vests placed over it, or use the crossbar of a mini or five-a-side goal.

Players have to control the ball at all times in this drill and ensure that the pass over the net keeps the ball on the court and in play. The coach can impose restrictions and rules to help improve certain ball control techniques. For instance, allowing only two touches per player; asking for the ball to be headed over; or specifying that each player in the team touch the ball before it is passed over.

Control and shoot

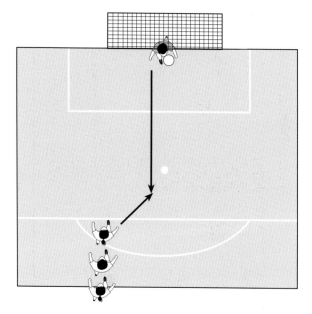

This is another great training ground exercise. It incorporates many techniques and competition for the players, with shot-stopping and angles for the goalkeeper. Players line up on the edge of the "D." The goalkeeper kicks or throws a ball in the air to the next player, who has to control the ball using one or more of the techniques and shoot to score from no closer than the penalty spot. The coach can decide how many and which control techniques are used.

The ball can bounce to start with, but as players become more adept they should be encouraged to volley the ball before it touches the ground. As an alternative, the coach, rather than the goalkeeper, can throw in the ball. Ask each player to retrieve any shots that are saved or that go high and wide.

Coaching Tip

Keep the teams to a maximum of four against four and have several games going on at once rather than all the players on one big court. This allows all players to stay warm and involved.

Progression 1 – Control and change of direction

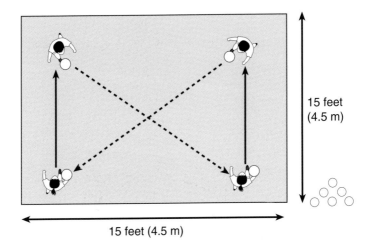

15 feet (4.5 m)

15 feet (4.5 m)

Player 1 throws the ball to player 2, who uses a certain ball control technique before passing/volleying to player 3 to catch. Player 3 throws the ball to player 4 who controls the ball before passing/volleying to player 1 to catch. Rotate the throwers so everyone has a turn. This teaches control and change of direction.

Progression 2 – Control, pass and move

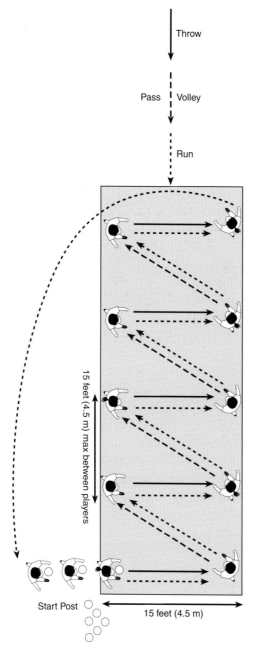

Throw

Pass | Volley

Run

15 feet (4.5 m) max between players

Start Post

15 feet (4.5 m)

If the team is particularly good at ball control you can join groups to have all players working in one session. Introduce a second and third ball to ensure none of the players get cold and they are always working with a ball. Each player takes the place of the player they have just thrown the ball to or volleyed to. The last player runs around the square to position 1 and starts the process again. Remember, you must have two or more players at the starting post. Play for 2 minutes before a minute's rest and recovery break.

Turning

Once players have received the ball and controlled it, they need to move off with it as fast as possible before an opponent can challenge them. They improve their chances of doing this effectively if they can turn quickly and sharply, so it is worth coaching your team in several turns to outwit your opponents. These should be adapted for left-footed players. Get your young players to practice these turns as often as possible – in the backyard, at the playground, in games – so that they take responsibility for their progress.

Coaching Tip

When players practice turns there are three major do's:
- start slowly
- bend knees
- accelerate away

For the following techniques, set up a square to an appropriate size for the number of players you are coaching. A good guideline is 10 feet × 10 feet (3 m × 3 m) per player. Give all the players a ball and ask them to move around the square practicing the moves and turning techniques that the coach calls out. Work for about two minutes on each technique. Finish the exercise by allowing the players to use any turning technique they choose.

Turning Away

A player receives the ball and tries to turn immediately and take off in another direction. If they keep running in the same direction, it is too easy for an opponent to guess where the ball will go next, allowing the opponent to catch and attempt to tackle them. The player reaches and hooks to turn the ball, trying not to run around the ball. They work on moving the ball on the turning touch back in the direction they want to go. A good drill for practicing this is for two players to pair up 30 feet (9 m) apart, each with a ball. The players move with the ball toward each other, and as they get closer they turn and move away again.

The Outside Hook

This is a simple technique to teach and learn. To begin the turn, a player reaches across the body and hooks the ball at the bottom with the outside of their foot. They sweep the ball around to the side with the same foot, leaning in the direction they want to go. The player turns to follow the path of the ball and accelerates away from their opponent as quickly as possible. They must not run around the ball. The ball is moved on the turning, touching it well in front of them and back in the direction they want to go.

The Inside Hook

As a player receives the ball, they watch out for approaching opponents and lean in the direction they want to go. The shoulder is dropped so that the player is partly turned. Then they hook the inside of the foot around the ball and move off at a sharp angle, dragging the ball with them and accelerating away.

The Drag Back

This is an ideal technique if a player is being closely marked. The player draws their leg back as if they were about to kick the ball, but swing their foot over it instead. As they bring the leg back again, they catch the top of the ball with their studs and drag the ball back, beginning to spin on their other foot. The player leans in the direction they want to go. When they have pulled the ball back, they complete the turn and accelerate away from their opponent.

The Maradona Turn

The Maradona turn, one of the most exciting skills in the game, is named after the great Argentinian soccer star, Diego Maradona. In this technique, the player steps on the ball with one foot and, as they come off the ball, swivel and drag the ball with the other foot. Their momentum will carry the ball with them, allowing them to continue to move forward.

The Cruyff Turn

This technique is named after the Dutch international, Johan Cruyff. This turn and other turning skills should form an essential part of any soccer coaching program. In the Cruyff turn, the ball is played between the legs, so that it ends up on the opposite side to that expected by the defender. With the ball on their right foot, the player positions themselves as if they were going to turn to the left, or to pass or cross the ball to the left. Then the player flicks the ball between their legs, and makes a quick turn to gather the ball. Usually, if they are using the right foot to send the ball behind them, they will turn in on their left side. The turn should be a quick pivot.

Throw-ins

Throw-in techniques and tactics are some of the more neglected skills in soccer. With the correct technique, effective training drills and some tactical awareness, a team can make much better use of throw-in opportunities during a game.

The throw-in technique starts by gripping the ball firmly but comfortably. The ball is brought back over the head, and the back is arched. Using the full extent of the arms and the power of the back and shoulders, the ball is released *in front of* the head. The feet position is a matter of personal preference with some players standing square and others placing one foot in front of the other. The final ingredient is to add a short run to generate rhythm and momentum.

Coaching Tips: The Basic Throw-in

- Stand facing the field with feet apart.
- Place one hand on each side of the ball but slightly behind the ball and form a "W" with your fingers well spread.
- Take the ball behind the head and throw forward onto the field.

Remember:

- Both feet must stay on the ground.
- Players can stand on or behind the side line.
- The ball must go behind the head.
- Players must use both hands equally.
- Beginners should throw toward the other team's goal.

Throw-in tactics depend on where the throw is being taken from. In the attacking third of the field, the objective is to get the ball into the penalty area as soon as possible, either by a direct throw or by creating an opening for a cross. In the middle third, the tactic should be to make forward runs. In the defensive third, the team must play safe, and try to create space to clear the ball away from danger. Useful tactics for creating space are overlapping runs, sudden changes of direction and decoy runs. A decoy run could take a marker away from the player who would like to receive the throw.

A good way to practice throw-ins is to line your team up in a row shoulder-to-shoulder and get them to practice their form without a ball. On the word "go," they should all pretend to make a throw-in while you watch. Comment and get them to do it again. Be sure they drag the toe of their rear foot, that their hands go behind their head and that they are upright and follow through with both arms.

When coaching throw-ins, look out for these common mistakes:

- Lifting a foot off the ground before the ball has left your hands (this is why it is important to drag the toe of the rear foot).
- Using one hand too much (the assistant referee can call this if it is obvious or if there is a lot of sidespin on the ball).
- Not taking the ball behind the head.

Positional Play

When looking at coaching basic skills, it is also worth mentioning how to play in the key positions in soccer:

- Goalkeeper
- Defender
- Attacker

Goalkeeping Basics

All players should have the opportunity to develop goalkeeping skills, particularly the 6 to 9 age group. And let them have fun while they are doing it.

Most young children see the goalkeeper's role as one of being on the goal line, stopping the shots. And they are right! Positional skills, such as narrowing the angle or coming off the line to field a crossed ball, can be encouraged but only once a budding goalkeeper has got the basics right. Children up to the age of 10 are not yet ready for that level of goalkeeping.

Catching the ball

The first skill that young players usually find difficult is catching the ball in the correct fashion. The keeper should always present both palms of the hands outward to the incoming ball in a "W" formation. This catching technique is unique to soccer goalkeeping and is the place to start their coaching.

Diving

A soccer goalkeeper needs a specific diving technique, unlike that of any other sport or gymnastic movement. Initially, most players will be reluctant to dive, so a graduated progression is needed. Everything will turn out fine in the end because we know children love to tumble and fall.

Throwing

Throwing a soccer ball is not easy for children with small hands and a lack of strength, especially if the wrong type and size of ball is used. I recommend a size 3 for children up to 10 years of age and a size 4 ball for those aged 10 to 14. Never use the size 5 ball before someone reaches 15 years of age. Throws should be underhand if played short, or from behind the shoulder (overhand) if looking to get distance quickly. The ball should be protected with the hand behind it when throwing.

Kicking

Kicking is invariably a problem for young goalkeepers. They very seldom get distance, and it often takes years of practice to get the timing and coordination right, especially for drop-kicks. It is simply a case of practice makes perfect.

What coaches should avoid, particularly in mini soccer, is always getting the "big kid" with the big kick to take the goal kicks. Simply try and coach your goalkeeper to play safe. Coach the team to accommodate the inability of the goalkeeper to kick long. Perhaps this means coaching your defenders to move wide for a short pass.

Organizing

It is important to encourage young goalkeepers to be the eyes and ears of the rest of the team. They have a full view of the field and can see the actions, movements and runs of players. This means goalkeepers can issue instructions to their teammates that will help shut down attacks against the team or create a quick counterattack. The basic message is to teach goalkeepers early on that they should be talking throughout the game in a positive way to their teammates.

Additionally, coaches should encourage goalkeepers to communicate clearly and concisely with their teammates. Goalkeepers should shout loudly but positively if they want the ball cleared or if they are confident that they will catch, kick or receive the ball. A simple instruction of "away" or "mine" is normally sufficient.

Goalkeeping drills

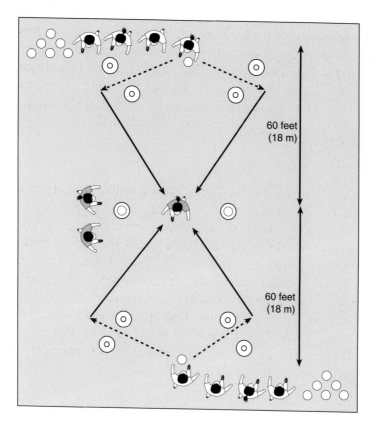

One particularly good drill for older players (aged 9 and up) is to place two pylons or cones as a goal in the middle of the training square. Have two sets of players each side of the goal, 50–60 feet (15–18 m) away. Rotating the strikers from each side, get them to knock the ball out of their feet and strike at goal. Once the shot has been made, a player from the opposite side does the same. In this drill the goalkeeper sees plenty of action and is thoroughly warmed up. To progress, get the strikers to take the ball wide through the cones to practice shooting from wide angles. This also allows the goalkeeper to practice positional skills.

NOTE: Change the goalkeeper after six or eight shots. If you have only one goalkeeper, let them do one minute of activity then rest for a minute and stretch for 30 seconds.

Defending Basics

The main purpose of a defender or defending team is to stop the opponents from attacking. There are many ways to do this, and it should always be remembered that defending starts from the moment the opposition gets the ball.

Jockeying

Jockeying – delaying the opponents – allows teammates to get into stronger positions and stop progress by the opposition. Teamwork is important and it should be the whole team's responsibility to defend when necessary and to win the ball back again.

Closing down opponents

Players must know how to close down an opponent quickly if they are approaching the goal. They must be careful not to close in too quickly or their opponent will use this to their advantage and swerve or fake their way past them. Encourage players to approach the player with the ball at a controlled speed, sideways on and slightly crouched to improve center of gravity. Get them to keep their eyes firmly on the ball, not on the opponent. They should be light on their toes to effect a quick adjustment should their opponent change direction. Players must be aware of the calls from supporting teammates – communication is vital when defending.

Interception

Interception is a good way of winning the ball back. This technique requires good anticipation, timing and teamwork. Encourage players to look at the way an opponent is shaping to make a pass and to try to get into a space where the ball is going before it gets there. Players should time their run to try and receive the ball in a way that allows them to carry on with momentum toward the opponent's goal. If teammates are pressuring the opponent with the ball, forcing them to make a hurried pass, then the opportunity to counterattack is increased and improved.

Clearing the ball

Clearing the ball is a priority for defending, especially from inside the goal area. It is not always possible to find the time or space in the area to control the ball and pick out an accurate pass to a teammate, so a quick clearance is the only option. The priority for clearing the ball, whether it be a kick, a header or a goalkeeper's punch, is to get the ball high, long and wide. This provides the time to regroup and "get shape back" while putting the ball out of the danger zone.

Playing "out of defense"

There may be times when players do have time on the ball when defending. This is the perfect opportunity for playing out of defense (counterattacking) and is a great way to catch the opposition off-guard. On the training ground, work on defenders playing a crisp pass to the feet of attackers, who lay the ball off to supporting midfielders. The midfielders should try and get the ball wide immediately and then continue their run to support the attackers or move on to the end of a cross.

Goalkeepers, too, should look to counterattack at the first opportunity. A quick throw or an accurate kick can suddenly create a counterattack.

Marking

Marking is another element of defending that requires regular practice. One-to-one marking means players pick up responsibility for staying close to a specific opponent throughout the game, staying goal-side of them all the time. The defender seldom allows the opponent to dwell or have time on the ball. This is particularly effective when you know that a particular player is a dangerous game-winning opponent.

Many teams adopt a sweeper system, which theoretically eliminates a one-on-one situation arising in defense. The sweeper, as you would imagine, picks up any loose ball that comes free in the defending area. The sweeper allows the central defender and fullbacks to concentrate on marking attackers. See which system works best for your team. You may need to adapt your defensive strategy and formation to suit the way the game is going.

Defending corners and free kicks

This is another important element that requires regular practice and good teamwork. These are two of the most dangerous situations for a defending team, and to defend successfully requires discipline and confidence. Players must be alert to the many options their opponents might adopt, such as a short corner, pass into midfield, near- and far-post cross. Get players to remember the golden rules: be alert, be confident and be first to the ball.

Tackling

Tackling is an essential skill because any team must be able to win the ball. If players cannot tackle, they are left relying on intercepting passes when opponents make a mistake. Tackling allows players to compete for the ball and take the initiative.

Beginners should start with the block tackle before learning the sliding tackle.

The block tackle starts by planting the nontackling foot firmly on the ground to provide a firm anchor. The inside of the foot is used for tackling, not the toe, and it is important to put the full weight of the body behind the ball, and to get the head down over the ball.

As with any tackling skill, timing is crucial. Players should try to tackle when their opponent is off-balance, or lets the ball go too far in front of them. This is often called "showing too much of the ball." Another good time to tackle is when an opponent looks down at the ball.

The sliding tackle or recovery tackle is an essential soccer skill requiring timing and technique. It is not only defenders who need to be able to tackle. Even forwards should be able to make a sliding tackle. It is best to tackle with the foot farthest from the ball. This gives extra reach and reduces the chances of giving away a foul. The sliding tackle is best made from a square position with the leg going out to the side rather than straight in front.

Timing is vital, and it takes plenty of practice to get it right. The key factors for any player are to watch the ball carefully, try to anticipate their opponent's move without being distracted, and always to go for the ball. If a player gets a foot on the ball first there is no foul, but if they miss the ball they will give away a free kick or be "left for dead."

A drill for the recovery tackle is for one player, acting as winger, to run with the ball down a narrow lane toward the touchline. They are given a head start over the defender, who chases after them and tries to make a sliding tackle, putting the ball into touch. The winger must try to reach the touchline without being tackled.

Attacking Basics

Whenever a team has possession of the ball, they are in attack, whatever the position of play. To play good attacking soccer, a team must combine all the skills of passing, movement and support in a positive and assertive way. The object is to get into a position to strike at the goal as quickly as possible.

These are just some of the fundamentals of good attacking play:

- good communication
- supporting the player with the ball
- making effective runs into space to take defenders away or to receive the ball
- choosing passes that find teammates
- using wall passes or one-twos
- making crossover runs with teammates to make play unpredictable
- passing crisply and accurately
- looking to play early passes
- not being afraid to shoot when the opportunity arises, and making shots accurate

Shooting

Without shooting at the goal, players won't score goals; and goals win games. Shooting is all about good technique, confidence and taking opportunities. Make sure players always make an attempt if they see an opportunity. Encourage them not to worry that they might miss, but to try to get the shot on target. They should always try and make the goalkeeper work and vary their shots, trying long- and short-range shots, chips and drives. Players should be alert when their teammates shoot – a rebound can always happen. Shots should be low and aimed for bottom corners away from the goalkeeper.

chapter 7

GAMES

Having introduced basic skills to young players in a structured manner, we now need to see them express themselves in live activity. The best way for a coach to see a child's development, and for the child to show off their newfound skills, is in a fun game situation. This chapter provides coaches with some ideas for introducing lively and fun games into a coaching session. The games are progressive so that each moves on to another, more technical one, or a game that extends their skills.

The one-hour coaching session agenda:

- warm up with a ball (10 minutes)
- coach a basic skill (15 minutes)
- introduce a fun game that allows players to use the new skill (10 minutes)
- play small-sided games that involve all the players (20 minutes).

With registration and drink breaks, your packed, hour-long session will fly by.

Fun games that teach skills

NOTE: Some of the games listed are "knockout" games where the last player left is the winner. Since the first ones knocked out are often the ones who need the most practice, those knocked out should be required to do something either to get back into the game or to keep them working on their ball skills until the game is over. One way around this that I find particularly effective is to let them become the chasers, or an equally important job in the drill. Games are grouped into skill categories, with each game teaching players a new aspect of soccer, such as dribbling, juggling and passing.

"The Coach Says" (5–7 years)

60 feet
(18 m)

60 feet (18 m)

Purpose
To encourage children to run with the ball, keeping it close to their feet.

Area needed
60 feet × 60 feet (18 m × 18 m).

Action
When the coach says "Stop – foot on the ball" (or replaces "foot" with "knee," "sit" or "elbow") the children must do so right away. The coach can also integrate commands such as change direction, go faster and so on. No one is eliminated from the game.

Equipment
Eight cones to mark the area and one ball per child.

Organization

Mark out a 60-foot × 60-foot (18 m × 18 m) area using the cones. The coach should start by demonstrating what each command means and ensure that all players understand these. Ask each child to dribble around the area with the ball remaining close to the foot.

Progression

The children have begun the process of dribbling. The next step would be to encourage them to use their peripheral vision. The next drill, "Beware the Tiger," will help this.

"Beware the Tiger" (8 years and over)

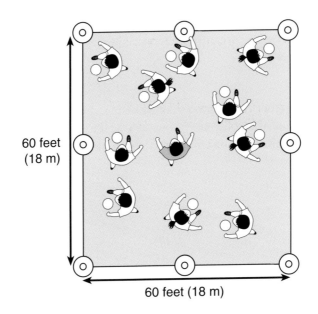

60 feet
(18 m)

60 feet (18 m)

Purpose
To encourage children to look up while dribbling at speed, using their peripheral vision in a controlled, pressurized and fun situation.

Area needed
60 feet × 60 feet (18 m × 18 m), for around 10 players.

Action
One child volunteers to be the tiger who prowls the jungle (the area) and tries to kick the soccer ball away from one of the other jungle animals and into the swamp (outside the area). If the tiger kicks a ball into the swamp, the tiger can retrieve it and become a different jungle animal with a ball. The child whose ball was kicked away is now the tiger.

Equipment
Eight cones and a soccer ball for each child except the tiger.

Organization

Set out a 60-foot × 60-foot (18 m × 18 m) area with the cones. Ask the jungle animals to dribble around the jungle, without dribbling into each other or the swamp (the area outside the grid). Remind children of safety points regarding challenging for the ball.

Progression

The next coaching technique would be to change speed and direction while beating a defender. The following game, "Crabs on the Beach," will help to illustrate how to develop these techniques in a fun environment.

"Crabs on the Beach" (5–8 years)

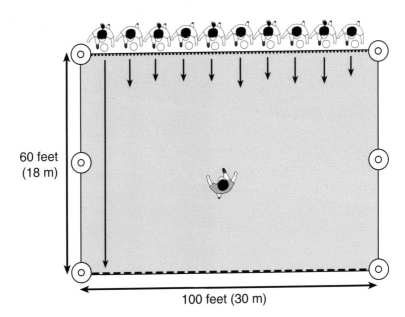

60 feet (18 m)

100 feet (30 m)

Purpose

To encourage children to dribble with the ball and change speed and direction to beat an opponent. The art of faking can be introduced at this stage.

Area needed

60-foot × 100-foot (18 m × 30 m) grid.

Action

Each child assumes the name of a sea creature, except the crab. Each creature has to run from the beach to the sea with a ball, avoiding the crabs who are trying to "pinch" the balls. A child whose ball is pinched then becomes a crab.

Equipment

Six cones and a soccer ball for each child except the crab.

Organization

Set out a 60-foot × 100-foot (18 m × 30 m) area with the cones. Make one 100-foot (30 m) line the sea and the other 100-foot (30 m) line the beach. Ask the children (sea creatures) to stand on the beach line, each with a foot on the ball. Place a child (the crab) in the middle of the area. On the coach's command, tell the creatures to dribble their ball from the beach to the sea while avoiding the crab. When they reach the sea line they must wait with a foot on the ball until all players have crossed the beach. The crab must aim to kick each child's soccer ball out of the grid via the 60-foot (18 m) sidelines. Any creatures losing their ball become a crab. The game continues on the coach's command with players now returning from the sea back to the beach. The last three children to be dribbling their balls become "sea champs."

"Numbers" or "Colors" (6 years and over)

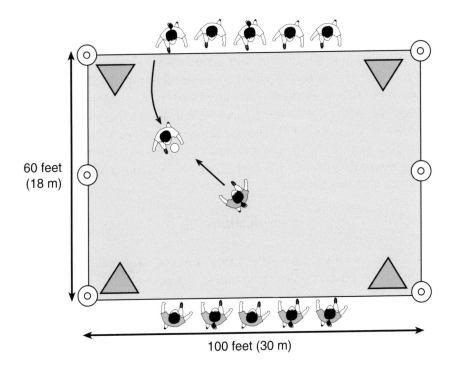

60 feet
(18 m)

100 feet (30 m)

Purpose
To encourage children to be confident to dribble in a one-against-one situation. This game is especially good on a hot day as the children defending can rest a bit.

Area needed
60-foot × 100-foot (18 m × 30 m) grid.

Equipment
Six cones, four pylons or poles as goalposts and a soccer ball.

Organization

Set out a 60-foot × 100-foot (18 m × 30 m) area with the cones. Divide the children into two groups. If you have 12 children, say, assign each child a number between 1 and 6 so that each team has a number 1, a number 2, and so on. Try to make sure the children with the same number are evenly matched. Set up two very wide goals with pylons. Spread six children on each side across each goal line. Call out one or more numbers, and those children come out to play 1 against 1, 2 against 2 and so on. The rest of the children stay spread across the goal line as defenders. Throw a ball from the sideline into the center and let them play it until a goal is scored or it goes out of bounds. If the opposing team gains possession of the ball, they become the attackers.

Coaching Tip

You could use two each of different colored vests, as younger children may have trouble remembering numbers.

"One in the Middle" (5 years and over)

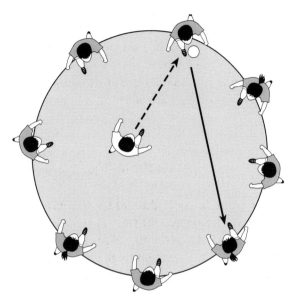

Purpose
To encourage children to shut the ball down and make the correct passing decision.

Area needed
A circle of players relevant to age and numbers.

Equipment
A soccer ball.

Organization

All players form a circle. One player goes in the center – this can be the coach if working with very young children (see tip below). The players forming the circle pass one ball among them while the person in the center tries to gain control of the ball. When this happens, the last player on the outside to touch the ball goes to the center. Some level of competitiveness develops but never on an individual basis. Do not allow the player in the middle to work for more than 30 seconds.

Coaching Tip

The coach may want to go in the center to start with but only to intercept a pass, never to tackle. This encourages players, especially the very young ones, to select a correct pass, and the coach can guide them by making it obvious. Make the circle tighter, relative to the players' ability. Sixteen-year-olds and above can play this on a one-touch basis.

Progression

Add a second or third defender in the middle to encourage greater speed of thought, decision, control and passing.

"Monster" (6–8 years)

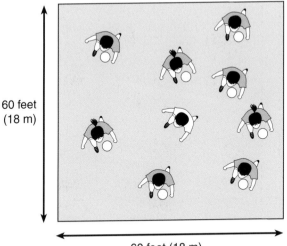

60 feet
(18 m)

60 feet (18 m)

Purpose
Ball control and protecting the ball.

Area needed
60 feet × 60 feet (18 m × 18 m).

Equipment
Eight cones to mark the area, a soccer ball for each player (except the monster) and a colored vest.

Organization
Mark off a 60-foot × 60-foot (18 m × 18 m) area for the game to be played and select one player to be the "monster." Get the rest of the children (each with a ball) to dribble around within the area. The monster attempts to touch each player on the shoulder or arm, at which point that player "freezes" with their foot on the ball. If a player's ball goes out of bounds, they also freeze. The last remaining unfrozen player gets to be the new monster for the next round.

"Kick Out" (6–8 years)

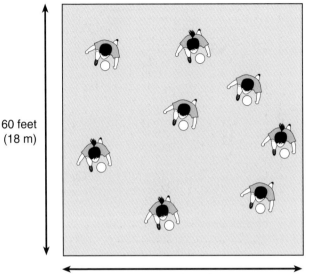

60 feet
(18 m)

60 feet (18 m)

Purpose
Ball control and protection.

Area needed
60 feet × 60 feet (18 m × 18 m).

Equipment
A soccer ball for each player.

Organization
Everyone dribbles and shields their ball within the area while trying to kick everyone else's ball out, and simultaneously protect their own. Players cannot kick someone else's ball out if their ball is not in the area. If their ball goes out they have to leave the area until it gets down to two children in a duel.

Coaching Tip

This game can end quite quickly, which is good for those eliminated early. However, the coach may need to reduce the area to achieve a quick ending.

"Give and Go" (8 years and over)

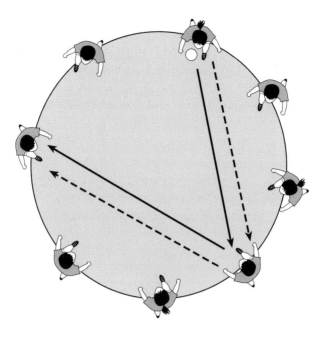

Purpose
This is good for getting the children to move after they make a pass.

Area needed
A circle of players, size depending on numbers, age and ability.

Equipment
One ball (minimum) and a distinctive colored vest.

Organization
Get the players to form a circle. Give the ball to one player and they call out someone's name and pass to them. They then run to the receiver's position in the circle. The receiver, on hearing their name called, steps forward to receive the pass and shouts their own name. The sequence is then repeated. Calling their own name out loud addresses the problem of players thinking someone else is getting the ball or pass. Players also learn each other's names quickly.

Coaching Tip

If the same players are involved and others left out, consider starting a countdown from 10 to 0 and get the players to figure out who has been left out (the left-out person should be quiet). They start yelling among themselves to figure out who it is, and this fosters communication on the field (it is pretty humorous too).

Progression

Once the players have grasped the game and the quality is improving, throw a second ball into the center. The players now have to think a bit more because two people are moving and two are busy with the balls.

"Simply Score" (6 years and over)

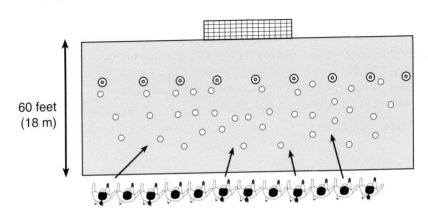

60 feet
(18 m)

Purpose
To encourage children to shoot at the goal and to gain greater appreciation of hitting the target rather than hitting a ball hard.

Area needed
An area appropriate in size to the age, ability and number of players; often this will be the goal area.

Equipment
More soccer balls than number of players, a goal and cones to mark the shooting line. If you decide to split the group into two teams in competition, vests will be required.

Organization

Mark a line 20 m from goal where players line up and a line of cones 15 feet (4.5 m) from goal to shoot from. Get the players to line up across one end of the area. Spread the balls out in front of them. Blow the whistle and turn the players loose. The object of the game is to get all the balls into the net as quickly as possible. They are all on the same team, and are not allowed to take a ball away from another player. Once a player has scored they turn and go back for another ball. Time them to see how fast they can accomplish the task. The children really like this game because they get to score a goal. The more balls the better.

Coaching Tip

Players must shoot from behind a line about 15 feet (4.5 m) from the goal. This stops players going into the goal and risking being hit by another shot.

"Marbles" (6 years and over)

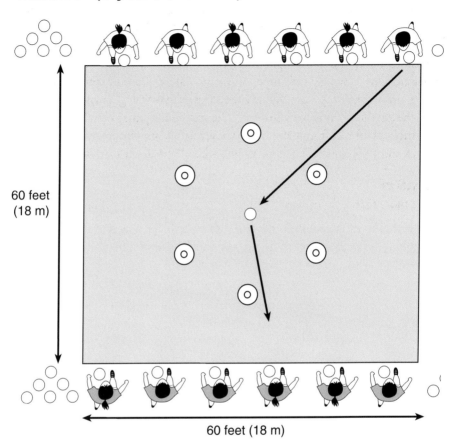

Purpose
To improve accuracy of passing.

Area needed
A rectangle or square appropriate in size to the age, ability and number of players.

Equipment
More soccer balls than players, a distinctive colored ball as the marble, cones to mark the center area and the touchlines.

Organization

Split your team into two groups and line them up behind two opposing lines, 60 feet (18 m) apart. Each player should have a ball. Place an unusual colored (or size) ball in the middle. This is the marble (a size 2 ball works well). Get the players to try to move the marble across the other team's line, or outside the inner circle of cones, by striking it with a ball. After the game starts, players are free to use any ball they can find. At first, the players may get really excited and kick the marble. If this happens, stop the game and put it back. Players must kick their soccer ball from behind their base line and use the correct passing style of kick (no toe-punts). The game is over when the ball exits the area.

Variation

Have more than one marble.

"Shark and Minnows" (6 years and over)

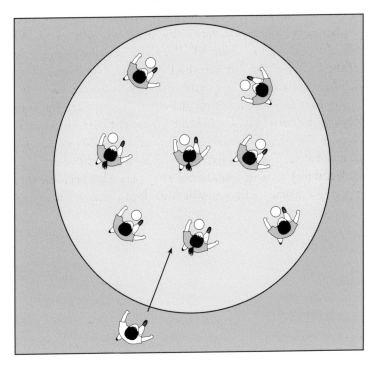

Purpose
This game teaches children with the ball to shield it from an opponent, and teaches children without the ball how to take an opponent's ball.

Area needed
A circle appropriate in size to the age, ability and number of players.

Equipment
A soccer ball for all players in the circle and a distinctive colored vest for the "shark."

Organization

Mark out a circle. One player, the shark, starts outside the circle without a ball. All other players, the minnows, start inside the circle with a ball. When the coach yells, "Shark's getting hungry!" the shark starts running around the outside of the circle and the fish start dribbling around inside the circle. When the coach yells, "Shark attack!" the shark enters the circle and has 30 seconds to send as many balls as possible outside the circle. When a ball leaves the circle for any reason, the corresponding fish must leave the circle and stay out until the coach gives the "Stop!" command at the end of the 30 seconds. A fish has done well if still alive. The shark has done well if very few fish survived. Choose a new shark and play another round until every player has been the shark once. Add competition as you see fit, i.e., which shark can kick the most balls away?

"Alamo" (7 years and over)

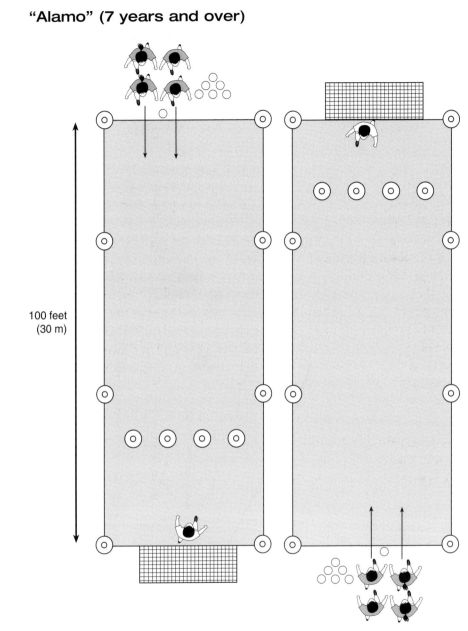

100 feet
(30 m)

Purpose
To encourage children to shoot at the goal and to gain greater appreciation of hitting the target rather than hitting a ball hard.

Area needed
An area appropriate in size to the age, ability and number of players; often this will be two lanes 100 feet (30 m) long × 30 feet (9 m) wide.

Equipment
Plenty of soccer balls on the goal line at each end, two goals, 16 cones to mark the areas, vests in two colors.

Organization
Mark two lanes 100 feet (30 m) long × 30 feet (9 m) wide (or as otherwise appropriate) side by side with a goal and a goalkeeper at one end of each lane (no goalkeeper if players are under 8). Create two teams in different vests. Line up the teams on opposite ends. They each have a ball. On the whistle, the first two players on each side dribble the ball, make quick passes to a point 15 feet (4.5 m) from the goal and shoot the ball into the goal. They then get the ball out of the goal and run to the back of the line coming the other way. Ask players to cheer their teammates. This can be a good team competition by adding up each team's score.

"Explode" (6 years and over)

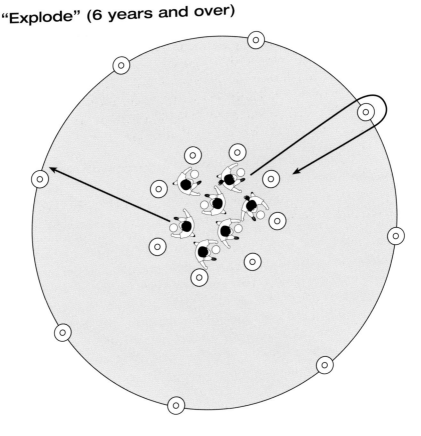

Purpose
To encourage children to maintain control of their ball while moving at a fast pace.

Area needed
Two circles of cones – one inner and one outer – size relevant to age and number of players.

Equipment
A soccer ball for each player.

Organization

Lay out an inner and outer ring of cones. Ask the players to dribble their ball in the inner circle. Make sure they use the insides of both feet. Make them keep control of the ball – always within one step – and do not let them run into one another or dribble their ball into another ball or another player. Keep telling them to keep their heads up and see the open spaces. On the shout "Explode!" the players all run away (dribbling their balls) as fast as they can. The first one to get to a boundary cone with their foot on the ball and their arm raised is the winner.

Progression

Players explode out, go around an outer cone and run back to the inner circle. The first one back with their foot on the ball and their arm raised is the winner.

"Slalom/Dribble Relay" (7 years and over)

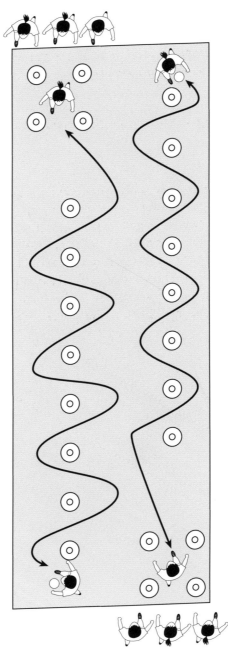

Purpose
Ball control at a fast pace.

Area needed
Two lines of cones in an area 60 feet (18 m) long × 30 feet (9 m) wide. Increase this to 100 feet (30 m) long for players 11-years-old and up.

Equipment
Two soccer balls and 24 cones – 16 for the slaloms and 8 for target "home" zones.

Organization
Set up an obstacle course with cones as "gates." Split the group into team A and team B. Each player takes it in turn to race against a player from the other team. If a player loses control or misses a gate, they have to regain control and go back through the gate. The final pass must go to the next player waiting in a target zone. A variation is to have a small square at each end. Players have to stop the ball in the square, then sprint back and high five the next player before they can take off. Players waiting their turn must stay in the square until their teammate returns. Add more cones and gates as the players improve their dribbling technique and skill.

"Red Light/Green Light" (6–8 years)

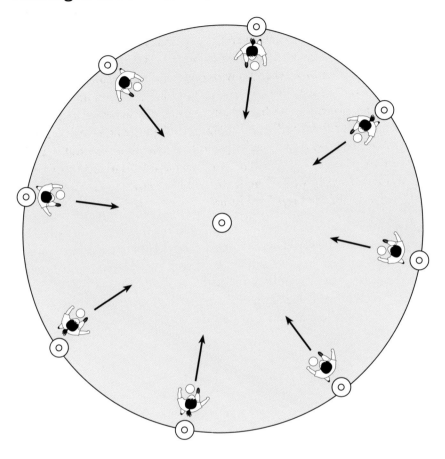

Purpose

To encourage children to dribble with the ball and change speed while retaining control of the ball.

Area needed

A large circle around 100 feet (30 m) in diameter.

Equipment

Cones to mark the outer edge of the circle, a soccer ball for each child, a large traffic-type cone or pole.

Organization

Each player with a ball waits on the edge of a big circle. Place a large traffic cone or pole in the middle as the target. The objective is for the players to dribble their ball to the traffic cone. However, the players can only move when the coach shouts, "Green light." The children race across the circle to see who can reach the traffic cone first. After a few seconds, the coach shouts, "Red light." At that command the players must stop and put a foot on top of the ball. The coach looks for players whose ball is still moving. Those players must move a certain distance back toward the starting line. Repeat calling red light/green light until someone wins the race by placing their hand on the traffic cone or pole, with their foot on the ball. The coach can add a bit of fun by calling out other words beginning with G or R to trick the players, such as "Go," "Get ready," "Right," "Ready break" or "Run."

"Dribbler's Alley" (9 years and over)

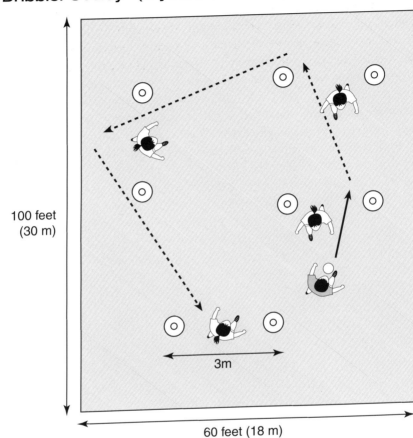

100 feet
(30 m)

3m

60 feet (18 m)

Purpose
To encourage children to dribble past opponents in order to score.

Area needed
60-foot × 100-foot (18 m × 30 m) grid.

Equipment
Six cones to mark the outer area, eight cones to mark four goals and a soccer ball for each attacker.

Organization

You need four or more players. Set up four goals/gates using the cones. Each goal should be 10 feet (3 m) wide, and there should be at least 10–15 feet (3–4.5 m) between each one. Each player guards a goal, and the remaining players try to dribble through it. The winner is the player who gets through the most goals without being tackled.

"The Hunter" (9 years and under)

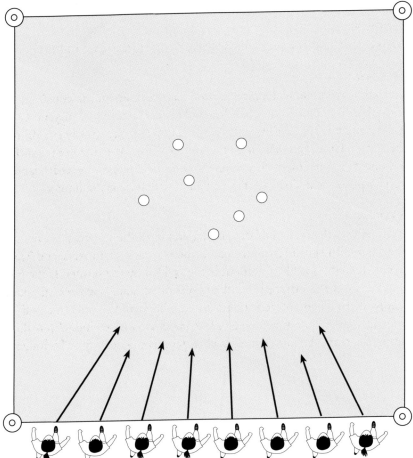

Purpose

To encourage children to dribble with the ball and change speed and direction to beat an opponent. To help them learn the art of protecting their ball from others.

Area needed
60-foot × 100-foot (18 m × 30 m) grid.

Equipment
Cones to mark the area of play. One soccer ball fewer than the number of players.

Organization
In this high-activity game, all players stand at a cone about 20 feet (6 m) from a group of balls. There is one ball fewer than the number of players. On the coach's command, the players run to the balls, get one and begin dribbling within a grid. The player who does not get a ball becomes the hunter and tries to steal one from the others. After a preset period has passed, the coach stops the game. The player who does not have a ball at that time is the hunter.

Progression
Place the balls at the far end of the playing area with the players lined up on the opposite line. On the coach's command, the players race to retrieve a ball and try to return to the start line without being tackled by the hunter. If the hunter steals a ball from the other player, the player dispossessed becomes the hunter. Play stops when all the players with a ball are back on the start line with their foot on the ball and an arm raised. Add competition by seeing who is the best hunter in the team. Ensure that all players get an opportunity to be hunters.

"Tag" (7 years and over)

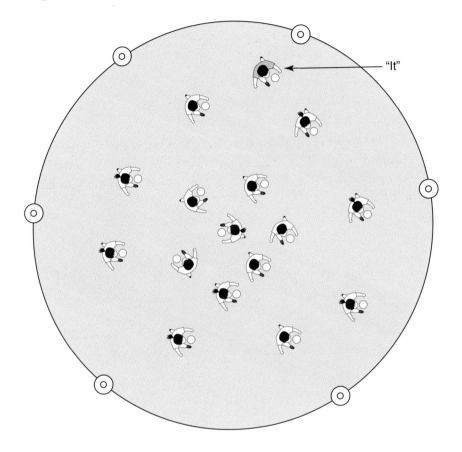

"It"

Purpose
Maintaining control of the ball while under pressure.

Area needed
Large circle or square, maximum 120 feet × 120 feet (37 m × 37 m) grid.

Equipment
Cones to mark the outer edge of the playing area. A soccer ball for everyone.

Organization

This drill is based on the common children's game of tag. Mark off a grid or circle. Everybody needs a ball. One player volunteers to be "it." Whoever is "it" must dribble to another player and tag them. The other player avoids being tagged by dribbling away from "it." If the player being chased loses their ball outside the grid, dribbles out of the grid or is tagged, they become "it" and the game continues.

Progression

"Ball tag." Everyone has a ball and dribbles in a confined area. The player who is "it" must pass their ball so that it hits another player's ball. The player whose ball is hit then becomes "it" but cannot hit the ball of the player who has just hit their ball.

"Snake" (6–8 years)

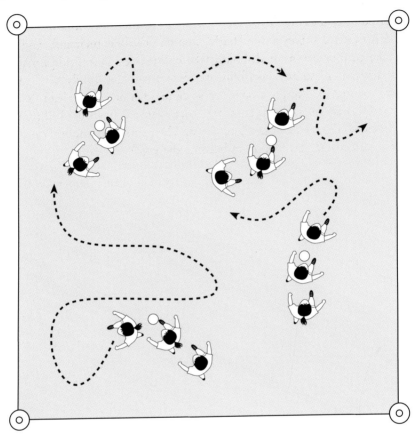

Purpose

To teach coordination, teamwork and basic ball control skills.

Area needed

120 feet × 120 feet (37 m × 37 m).

Equipment

Four cones to mark out the area. A soccer ball for each group of three.

Organization

Players are grouped into threes (preferred) or fours. The first player is the "head" of the snake and does not have a ball. They are the leader in a follow-the-leader game. The second player is the "body" and has a ball at their feet, and must follow the head of the snake, dribbling wherever they go. The third player is the "rattle" without a ball and just following. Encourage the "heads" to vary their lead by moving fast, slow, sideways and stopping. Let one player lead for about 20 seconds. Then, on a whistle from the coach, player 2 leaves the ball for player 3 and becomes the head of the snake. Player 3 becomes the body and the former head of the snake circles around to become the rattle.

"Decision Time" (8 years and over)

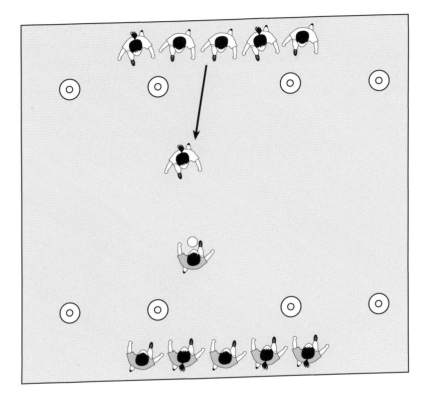

Purpose
To develop confidence in taking on and beating an opponent.

Area needed
60 feet × 60 feet (18 m × 18 m).

Equipment
Eight cones to create four goals. Six soccer balls.

Organization

Place two small goals on one side of a grid and two goals opposite. Split the players into two groups and give them a number: one, two, three and so on. The coach throws a ball into the center and calls out a number. The corresponding players play one against one, trying to score through either of the opponent's goals. This can be a competitive team game – first player or team to five or 10 goals.

"Circle Game" (6 years and over)

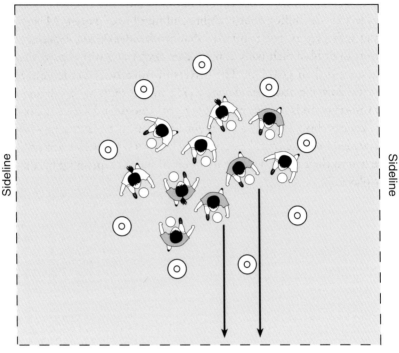

Goal line

Purpose
Keeping control of the soccer ball under pressure.

Area needed
100-foot × 100-foot (30 m × 30 m) square with an inner circle of cones.

Equipment
Four cones to mark the area of play plus enough cones to mark an inner circle. A soccer ball for all players.

Organization

Set up a grid, from 60 feet × 60 feet (18 m × 18 m) to 100 feet × 100 feet (30 m × 30 m) in size, depending on age, ability and number of players. Make a center circle and split players into two teams that can be identified by a color. Get all the players to dribble their balls in the center circle. Call out a color. That team dribbles toward their goal line. The players in the other team leave their balls and run to slow the attackers down, trying to get them to a sideline and to dribble out-of-bounds, or not get to their goal line before the coach counts to seven. Coaches should award a point for each out-of-bounds and a point for each player held for the coach's count. Attackers get a point for each player who gets the ball to their goal line. Play to 10 or 20 points depending on the ability of your players.

"Keeping the Ball" (6 years and over)

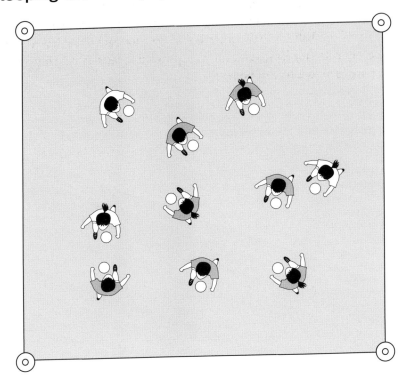

Purpose
Keeping control and protecting the ball.

Area needed
60 feet × 60 feet (18 m × 18 m).

Equipment
Four cones to mark the area. A soccer ball for all players.

Organization

Everyone dribbles around, trying to keep their own ball and kick out everyone else's ball. If a player's ball is kicked out, they must retrieve it then toe-tap or box-the-ears of the ball for 10 touches before getting back in. A player gets a point for every ball they kick out (so if you spend time outside dancing on your ball, you have less time to win points).

"Maps" (8 years and over)

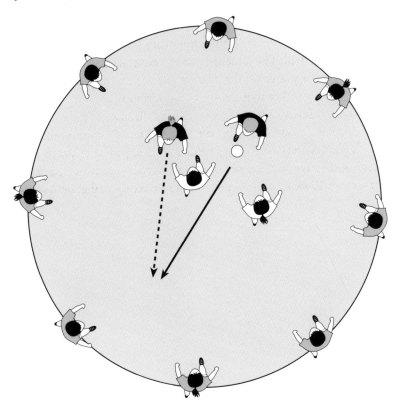

Purpose
This drill teaches awareness of Movement, Availability, Pace and Space – MAPS.

Area needed
Circle of players, the size dependent on numbers, ability and ages.

Equipment
One soccer ball and four vests in two different colors.

Organization

Players form a circle. One of the players on the outside has the ball. Four players work inside the circle, two designated as attackers and the other two as defenders. To start, an attacker in the center calls for a pass from the player on the outside with the ball. The attacker looks to control the ball and pass to their teammate or another player on the outside but not the player they received the first pass from. An attacker then moves to a position where they can receive the ball and play continues. The defenders try to dispossess the attacker and, if successful, become the attacker. Play for a maximum of a minute then swap the players with players on the outside. The drill teaches players many aspects of the game such as effective movement, creation of space, receiving the ball, taking defenders "away," passing techniques, decision-making and good ball control.

Ball Juggling: "P-E-L-E" (8–11 years)

Purpose
To practice ball skills in pairs.

Area needed
Enough room to work with the ball.

Equipment
Each player needs a soccer ball (although two players can share one).

Organization
Divide the team into pairs. The first player keeps the ball up once using a part of the body. The second player has to mirror this. The first player then juggles twice, and the second player matches. The first player then juggles three times, and so on. When a player misses, the other player gets a letter: first "P" then "E" then "L" then "E." After awarding a letter, the players start out at one again. The first player to spell "PELE" is the winner. This can be played with thighs only, feet only, head only or any combination.

"The Juggler" (7–11 years)

Purpose
To practice ball skills in pairs.

Area needed
Enough room to work with the ball.

Equipment
Each player needs a soccer ball (although two players can share one).

Organization
Play with two or more players. The first player keeps the ball up with as many touches as they can and keeps track of count. The second player goes after the first miss. After the second player misses, the first player goes again, resuming the count from where they missed in their first turn. For example, if a player got five touches in their first turn, they would start the second turn at six. The first player to a specific number wins.

Progression
This game can be made more challenging by restricting it to certain body parts. For more experienced and skillful players who can keep the ball up with hundreds of touches, you can have both players working at the same time, counting out loud the number of touches they have. The winner is the first one to reach a certain number.

"Juggling with Movement" (9 years and over)

Purpose
Ball control on the move.

Area needed
Enough distance to move with the ball.

Equipment
One soccer ball (but the more the better) and a goal/target.

Organization
Players start at one spot and walk/jog/run while juggling the ball (no hands!). The aim is for players to see how far they can go without dropping the ball. A variation of this is to start at the outside of the penalty area on the field, juggle up to the goal area and shoot/volley the ball into the net without letting it hit the ground.

Progression
You could have a race between two more experienced and skillful players, or time them between two points before they shoot.

"Timed Juggles" (9–11 years)

Purpose
To see how many touches the player can get in a certain amount of time.

Area needed
Enough area to juggle a soccer ball.

Equipment
One soccer ball.

Organization
Do a two-minute timed contest. Initially the players do not have to keep the ball up without a miss. This is great for getting the players focused and working hard for a certain time period. It's also good for aerobic fitness.

"Team Juggling Contest" (7–11 years)

Purpose
To see how many touches a team can get in a certain amount of time.

Area needed
Enough for all players to line up and juggle a soccer ball facing their opponents.

Equipment
One soccer ball for each player.

Organization
Get each player to juggle and see how many touches they can get. Add the total touches for the whole team and create a team record. When the players are not very good jugglers, this game does not take very long. I have seen huge improvements in my teams' juggling skills by doing nothing more than this game. It is just enough focus to get them working on their own. Very young players can catch the ball at times. Ensure you ask them to practice at home and try to beat their record.

"Goalkeeper Wars" (8 years and over)

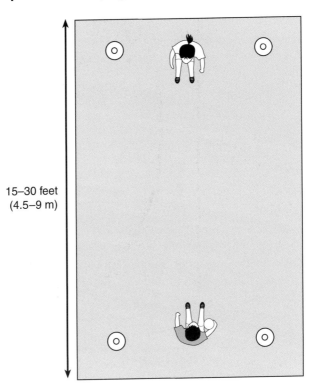

15–30 feet
(4.5–9 m)

Purpose
Goalkeeper warm-up.

Area needed
15–30 feet (4.5–9 m) long × 15 feet (4.5 m) wide.

Equipment
Four cones to create two goals, lots of soccer balls for both goalkeepers.

Organization
Using four cones, create two goals about 15–25 feet (4.5–8 m) apart (depending on players' age, ability and so on). The width of the goals should be just beyond the armspan of the goalkeepers. The goalkeepers sit just in front of the cones, facing each other. Each attempts to score goals by throwing the ball through the opponent's goal. The ball must be kept below their shoulders.

"Goalkeeper Rotations" (all ages)

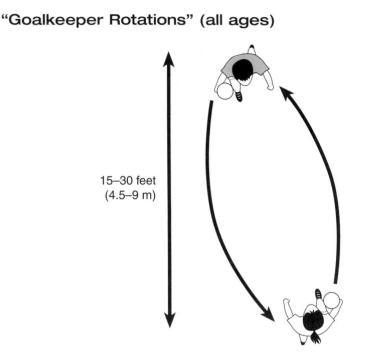

15–30 feet
(4.5–9 m)

Purpose
Goalkeeper warm-up.

Area needed
15 feet × 15 feet (4.5 m × 4.5 m).

Equipment
Two soccer balls of any size.

Organization
Two goalkeepers face each other, both with a ball. Using the right hand, they throw their ball to the other goalkeeper and continue the rotation, speeding up as they become more comfortable with the requirements of the game. Start each goalkeeper with, say, 5 points. The first one to drop their ball loses a point until there is a winner. Take a break, then start again using the left hand. Other variations include high and wide throws. You can also use a standard-size ball and a tennis ball to encourage alertness and flexibility.

"Penalty King" (8 years and over)

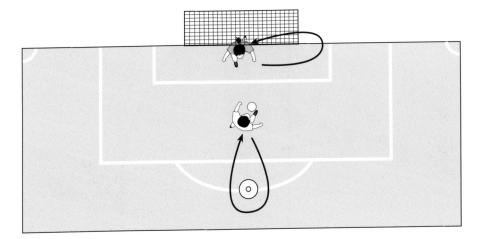

Purpose
To boost confidence, improve accuracy of shooting and goalkeeper's positioning and reflexes.

Area needed
The goal area; 30 feet × 30 feet (9 m × 9 m) up to 60 feet × 60 feet (18 m × 18 m), depending on age and ability of the players.

Equipment
Minimum two players (one goalkeeper), one goal, five soccer balls (minimum), one cone or pole.

Organization
Place the goalkeeper on the goal line and the ball on the penalty spot. Place a cone or pole 15–30 feet (4.5–9 m) back from the ball. On the word "Go" the goalkeeper runs around a goalpost or touches it, and prepares themselves to save the penalty while the striker turns and runs around the pole, and then strikes the ball. This continues without stopping for five penalties. To add competition, the striker only wins if they score three goals or more. Make sure you switch the goalkeepers and players regularly so they can rest and have a drink.

"Strike to Score" (9 years and over)

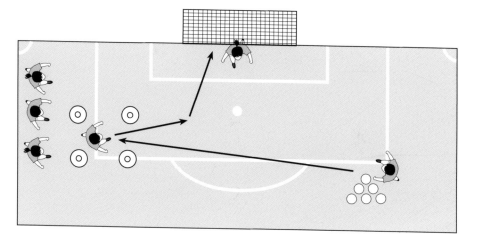

Purpose
Encourages passing, control, shooting and shot-stopping.

Area needed
18-yard area.

Equipment
Plenty of soccer balls, goal and four cones.

Organization
Place a 30-foot × 30-foot (9 m × 9 m) square marked by cones inside the penalty area on the corner of the 18-yard area. Have a stock of soccer balls outside the penalty box on the other side at the corner of the 18-yard area. Player 1 by the soccer balls passes a soccer ball to player 2 in the grid who controls with their first touch and strikes at goal with their second touch. To encourage a good first touch the ball cannot leave the grid. Player 2 now moves to the bunch of balls while player 1 goes around the goal to retrieve any shots and joins the group of strikers in the grid. Goalkeepers can take it in turn to stop the shot. The winner is the first player to score a certain number of goals or the goalkeeper to stop a certain number of shots.

Appendix 1

Useful Addresses

Soccer

American Youth Soccer Organization (AYSO)
AYSO National Support & Training Center
12501 South Isis Avenue
Hawthorne, California 90250
Tel: (800) 872-2976
Fax: (310) 643-5310
Website: www.soccer.org
AYSO is a nationwide nonprofit organization that develops and delivers youth soccer programs in a fun, family environment. AYSO runs the Very Important Player program, which aims to get children and adults with physical or mental disabilities involved in soccer, and Safe Haven, a program designed to protect children and the volunteers who work with them from abuse and harassment. AYSO also offers training and support to coaches. Links to all of AYSO's regional offices can be found on the website.

Canadian Soccer Association
Place Soccer Canada
237 Metcalfe Street
Ottawa, Ontario K2P 1R2
Tel: (613) 237-7678
Fax: (613) 237-1516
Email: mini@soccercan.ca
Website: www.canadasoccer.com
An affiliate of FIFA, Concacaf and the Canadian Olympic Association, the Canadian Soccer Association is Canada's premier soccer organization, dedicated to promoting soccer at all levels, from youth to international. They also offer certification programs for coaches of all levels. The website includes information on mini-soccer and links to Canada's provincial soccer associations, which administer youth soccer programs.

The Confederation of North, Central American and Caribbean Association Football (Concacaf)
Website: www.concacaf.com
Concacaf is one of six continental confederations of FIFA and serves as the governing body of soccer for the Americas. It is composed of 40 national associations, from Canada in the north to Surinam in the south.

Fédération Internationale de Football Association (FIFA)
FIFA-Strasse 20
P.O. Box 8044
Zurich, Switzerland
Tel: +41 43 222 7777
Fax: +41 43 222 7878
Website: www.fifa.com
FIFA is soccer's world governing body and is composed of 208 member associations. In addition to organizing soccer's World Cup, FIFA runs programs such as FIFA Ambassadors against Racism, which promotes racial tolerance, and Football for Hope, which uses soccer to support, advise and strengthen sustainable social and human development programs.

Major League Soccer (MLS)
Tel: (877) 557-3774
Email: feedback@mlsnet.com
Website: www.mlsnet.com
Founded in 1996, Major League Soccer is the top-flight professional soccer league in the United States. The league has 13 teams, including one based in Toronto, Canada.

National Soccer Coaches Association of America (NSCAA)
6700 Squibb Road, Suite 215
Mission, Kansas 66202
Toll-free tel: (800) 458-0678
Local tel: (913) 362-1747
Fax: (913) 362-3439
Website: www.nscaa.com
NSCAA is the largest coaches' organization in the United States, comprised of more than 23,000 members who coach both genders at all levels of the sport. It fulfills its mission of coaching education through a nationwide program of clinics and week-long courses, teaching more than 4,000 soccer coaches yearly.

National Soccer Hall of Fame and Museum
18 Stadium Circle
Oneonta, New York 13820
Tel: (607) 432-3351
Fax: (607) 432-8429
Website: www.soccerhall.org
The National Soccer Hall of Fame is a 40,000-square foot facility that houses the National Soccer Museum, the Hall of Fame and an interactive "Kicks Zone" game area. Kicks Zone allows visitors to see and hear the story of soccer in America in a hands-on and feet-on environment. The hall also houses an extensive archive of American soccer memorabilia.

U.S. Deaf Soccer Association
3711 Sout State Route 157
Glen Carbon, Illinois 62034
E-mail: ken_noll24@hotmail.com
Website: www.usdeafsoccer.com
An affiliate of the U.S.A. Deaf Sports Federation, the U.S. Deaf Soccer Association fields men's and women's teams at the Deaflympics.

U.S. Soccer Federation
1801 South Prairie Avenue
Chicago, Illinois 60616
Tel: (312) 808-1300
Fax: (312) 808-1301
Website: www.ussoccer.com
The governing body of soccer in all its forms in the United States, its mission statement is to make soccer, in all its forms, a preeminent sport in the United States and to continue the development of soccer at all recreational and competitive levels. The U.S. Soccer Federation offers development courses for elite athletes and intermediate and senior coaches.

U.S. Youth Soccer
Tel: (800) 4-SOCCER
Website: www.usyouthsoccer.org
U.S. Youth Soccer is a nonprofit educational organization that aims to provide a fun and healthy activity through recreational soccer programs and small-sided games. Every child is guaranteed playing time, and the game is taught in an enjoyable atmosphere. The Outreach Program for Soccer (TOPSoccer) is a community-based training and team-placement program for young athletes with disabilities that is designed to allow any child with a mental or physical disability to learn and play soccer. U.S. Youth Soccer offers coaching courses through each of its 55-member state associations, and the website includes links to its four regional sites and the state associations.

Women's United Soccer Association (WUSA)
Website: wusa.com
Established in 2001, WUSA was envisioned to be the world's premier women's professional soccer league. Despite attracting top players, it folded in 2003. Attempts were made to revive the league in 2004, and reports are circulating that WUSA will field eight teams in 2008, following the FIFA Women's World Cup.

General Sports and Fitness

Coaching Association of Canada (CAC)
141 Laurier Avenue West, Suite 300
Ottawa, Ontario K1P 5J3
Tel: (613) 235-5000
Fax: (613) 235-9500
Email: coach@coach.ca
Website: www.coach.ca
CAC is a nonprofit amateur sport organization with the mandate to improve the effectiveness of coaching across all levels of sports. They provide information on topics such as ethics, nutrition, training and certification and women in coaching.

The National Collegiate Athletic Association
700 W. Washington Street
P.O. Box 6222
Indianapolis, Indiana 46206-6222
Tel: (317) 917-6222
Fax: (317) 917-6888
Website: www.ncaa.org
The NCAA's core purposes are to govern competitions in a fair, safe, equitable and sportsmanlike manner and to integrate intercollegiate athletics into higher education so that the educational experience of the student-athlete is paramount. They also actively promote an inclusive culture that fosters equitable participation for student-athletes and career opportunities for coaches and administrators from diverse backgrounds.

The President's Council on Physical Fitness and Sports
Department W
200 Independence Avenue,
SW Room 738-H
Washington, District of Columbia
20201-0004
Tel: (202) 690-9000
Fax: (202) 690-5211
Website: www.fitness.gov
The President's Council on Physical Fitness and Sports is a committee of volunteer citizens who advise the president through the Secretary of Health and Human Services about physical activity, fitness and sports. Through its programs and partnerships with public, private and nonprofit sectors, the Council serves as a catalyst to promote health, physical activity, fitness and enjoyment for people of all ages, backgrounds and abilities through participation in physical activity and sports.

Sport Canada
16th Floor, 15 Eddy Street
Gatineau, Quebec K1A 0M5
Toll-free tel: (866) 811-0055
Local tel: (819) 956-8003
Fax: (819) 956-8006
Email: sportcanada@pch.gc.ca
Website:
www.pch.gc.ca/progs/sc/index_e.cfm
Sport Canada is a branch of the International and Intergovernmental Affairs and Sport Sector within the federal Department of Canadian Heritage. Their website includes information about funding programs and links to major sports organizations from across Canada.

Girls and Women

Canadian Association for the Advancement of Women and Sport and Physical Activity (CAAWS)
N202-801 King Edward Avenue
Ottawa, Ontario K1N 6N5
Tel: (613) 562-5667
Fax: (613) 562-5668
Website: www.caaws.ca
CAAWS's mission is to ensure that girls and women have access to a complete range of opportunities and choices and that they have equality as participants and leaders in sports and physical activity. They promote the values of equity, inclusiveness, fairness, and respect.

National Association for Girls & Women in Sport (NAGWS)
American Alliance for Health, Physical Education, Recreation & Dance
1900 Association Drive
Reston, Virginia 20191-1598
Toll-free tel: (800) 213-7193
Local tel: (703) 476-3400
Website: www.aahperd.org/nagw
The NAGWS's mission is to develop and deliver equitable and quality sport opportunities for all girls and women through relevant research, advocacy, leadership development, educational strategies and programming that promote social justice and change.

Women's Sports Foundation
Eisenhower Park
East Meadow, New York 11554
Toll-free tel: (800) 227-3988
Local tel: (516) 542-4700
Fax: (516) 542-4716)
Email: info@womenssportsfoundation.org
Website:
www.womenssportsfoundation.org
The Women's Sports Foundation aims to advance the lives of girls and women through sport and physical activity. Among their programs is It Takes A Team!, an educational campaign for lesbian, gay, bisexual and transgender issues that focuses on eliminating homophobia as a barrier to both women and men participating in sport.

Players with Disabilities

Active Living Alliance for Canadians with a Disability (ALACD)
720 Belfast Road, Suite 104
Ottawa, Ontario K1G 0Z5
Toll-free tel: (800) 771-0663
Local tel: (613) 244-0052
Toll-free TTY: (888) 771-0663
Local TTY: (613) 244-0008
Fax: (613) 244-4857
E-mail: info@ala.ca
Website: www.ala.ca
ALACD promotes, supports and enables Canadians with disabilities to lead active, healthy lives. They provide nationally coordinated leadership, support, encouragement, promotion and information that facilitate healthy, active living opportunities for Canadians of all abilities across all settings and environments.

Canadian Cerebral Palsy Sports Association (CCPSA)
305-1376 Bank Street
Ottawa, Ontario K1H 7Y3
Toll-free tel: (866) 247-9934
Local tel: (613) 748-1430
Fax: (613) 748-1355
Email: info@ccpsa.ca
Website: www.ccpsa.ca
CCPSA is an athlete-focused national organization that administers and governs sport opportunities targeted to athletes with cerebral palsy and related disabilities. Athletes compete at all levels, from local to international. The website includes information on the sports programs available, including soccer, and links to the provincial organizations that administer the programs.

Special Olympics
1133 19th Street, N.W.
Washington, District of Columbia 20036
Tel: (202) 628-3630
Fax: (202) 824-0200
Website: www.specialolympics.org
Special Olympics Canada
60 St. Clair Avenue East, Suite 700
Toronto, Ontario M4T 1N5
Tel: (416) 927-9050
Fax: (416) 927-8475
E-mail: info@specialolympics.ca
Website: www.specialolympics.ca
Special Olympics is an international nonprofit organization that is dedicated to empowering individuals with intellectual disabilities to become physically fit, productive and respected members of society through sports training and competition. Special Olympics offers children and adults with intellectual disabilities year-round training and competition in 30 Olympic-type summer and winter sports, including soccer.

Gay, Lesbian, Bisexual and Transgendered Players

Gay and Lesbian Athletes Association
70 East Beaver Creek Road, Suite 30
Richmond Hill, Ontario L4B 3B2
Tel: (905) 882-7046
Fax: (905) 882-7056
E-mail: info@glpaa.org
Website: www.glpaa.org
A registered charity operating in both the United States and Canada, GLAA aims to create an atmosphere where athletes can compete without concerns about sexual orientation. They offer a number of resource materials for coaches and athletes.

Child Protection and Safety

Canadian Centre for Child Protection Inc.
615 Academy Road
Winnipeg, Manitoba R3N 0E7
Toll-free tel: (800) 532-9135
Local tel: (204) 945-5735
Website: www.protectchildren.ca
The Canadian Centre for Child Protection is a charitable organization dedicated to reducing child victimization by providing programs and services to Canadians. Their child protection kit outlines child protection policies, recruitment and screening standards, a mechanism for identifying and reporting potential abuse and a guide for parents.

Child Welfare Information Gateway
Children's Bureau/ACYF
1250 Maryland Avenue SW, Eighth Floor
Washington, District of Columbia 20024
Toll-free tel: (800) 394-3366
Local tel: (703) 385-7565
Fax: (703) 385-3206
Email: info@childwelfare.gov
Website: www.childwelfare.gov
*A service of the Children's Bureau,
Administration for Children and Families,
U.S. Department of Health and Human
Services, the Child Welfare Information
Gateway provides access to print and
electronic publications, websites and online
databases covering a wide range of topics
from prevention to permanency, including
child welfare and child abuse and neglect.*

**National Sex Offender Public
Registry (NSOR)**
www.nsopr.gov
*The National Sex Offender Registry tracks
the whereabouts and movements of certain
convicted sex offenders. The National Crime
Information Center (NCIC) enables the
NSOR to retain the offender's current
registered address, dates of registration and
conviction, and residence. Members of the
public can check the NSOR, but some states
also maintain their own registries, and these
should be consulted as well. A list of state
registries can be found on the FBI's website
at www.fbi.gov/hq/cid/cac/states.htm.*

Royal Canadian Mounted Police
RCMP Headquarters
1200 Vanier Parkway
Ottawa, Ontario K1A 0R2
Website: www.rcmp-grc.gc.ca
*The RCMP provides information on
Canada's National Sex Offender Registry,
which is not open to members of the public.
The RCMP's website also provides links to
provincial police services.*

Volunteer Canada
330 Gilmour Street
Ottawa, Ontario K2P 2P6
Toll-free tel: (800) 670-0401
Local tel: (613) 231-4371
Fax: (613) 231-6725
Email: info@volunteer.ca
Website: www.volunteercanada.ca
*Volunteer Canada supports volunteerism and
civic participation through ongoing programs
and special projects and by developing
resources and national initiatives. They offer
a wealth of information about how to screen
volunteers, including a brochure entitled
"Understanding Police Records Checks."*

Health and Welfare

American Red Cross National Headquarters
2025 E Street, NW
Washington, DC 20006
Tel: (202) 303-4498
Website: www.redcross.org

Canadian Red Cross
National Office
170 Metcalfe Street, Suite 300
Ottawa, Ontario K2P 2P2
Tel: (613) 740-1900
Fax: (613) 740-1911
Email: feedback@redcross.ca
Website: www.redcross.ca
The Red Cross offers basic to advanced first-aid courses, covering everything from CPR and automated external defibrillator (AED) training, to how to treat shock, hypothermia, poisonings and muscle, bone and joint injuries.

St. John Ambulance
National Office
1900 City Park Drive, Suite 400
Ottawa, Ontario K1J 1A3
Tel: (613) 236-7461
Fax: (613) 236-2425
Website: www.sja.ca
St. John Ambulance offers first-aid courses in Canada. Topics covered include cardiovascular emergencies and CPR, emergency-scene management, choking, severe bleeding and shock, unconsciousness and fainting, medical conditions such as diabetes and asthma, child resuscitation, AED, bone and joint injuries, head/spinal and pelvic injuries, chest injuries, heat and cold illness and injuries, wound care and multiple casualty management.

Appendix 2

Further Reading

Buxton, Ted. *Soccer Skills for Young Players.* Buffalo, New York: Firefly Books, 2007.

Fédération Internationale de Football Association. *Laws of the Game.* Zurich, Switzerland: FIFA, 2006.

Herbst, Dan. *Soccer: How to Play the Game.* Compiled by U.S. Soccer staff. New York, New York: Universe, 1999.

Hunt, Chris, ed. *The Complete Book of Soccer.* Buffalo, New York: Firefly Books, 2006.

National Soccer Coaches Association of America. *The Soccer Coaching Bible.* Champaign, Illinois: Human Kinetics Publishers, 2004.

Saunder, Norman and Jeremy Friedman, eds. *Caring for Kids: The Complete Guide to Children's Health.* Buffalo, New York: Firefly Books, 2006.

Shepherd, John. *Sports Training: The Complete Guide.* Buffalo, New York: Firefly Books, 2007.

U.S. Youth Soccer. *The Official U.S. Youth Soccer Coaching Manual.* Frisco, Texas: U.S. Youth Soccer, 2002.

Appendix 3

SAMPLE RISK ASSESSMENT FORM

Risk assessment form

Venue/Date:
Name/position:

Playing/Training Area

Are areas free of dangerous obstacles? Is area fit and appropriate for chosen activity? (Tick appropriate response.)

Yes   No

Outline any hazards and detail what action was taken or will be taken:

Goalposts/other equipment

Are goalposts safe and appropriate for the activity? Yes   No

Outline any unsafe equipment, who may be at risk and what action was taken:

Players

Is the emergency contacts/medical registry completed and up-to-date?

Yes   No

Outline current state and what action was taken:

Is all the players' attire appropriate and safe for chosen activity?

Yes   No

Outline any unsafe equipment/attire and any action taken:

Emergency Access

Can emergency vehicles access areas safely and without obstacle?

Is telephone working?

Index

OKANAGAN REGIONAL LIBRARY
3 3132 02743 3228